Once Upon a Lifetime

A Teacher's-Eye View
of Living in the World Today

Craig E. Burgess

Craig E. Burgess
12/4/94

Noble House
Baltimore, Maryland

**Once Upon a Lifetime:
A Teacher's-Eye View of Living in the World Today**

Copyright © 1994 Craig E. Burgess

All rights reserved under International and Pan-American copyright conventions. No part of this book may be reproduced, stored in a retrieval system, or transmitted in any form, electronic, mechanical, or other means, now known or hereafter invented, without written permission. Address all inquiries to the publisher.

Library of Congress
Cataloging in Publication Data
ISBN 1-56167-147-9

Published by

Noble House
A Division of American Literary Press

8019 Belair Rd, Ste 10
Baltimore, Maryland 21236

Manufactured in the United States of America

Dedication

This collection of poems is dedicated to all of the students from Cherry Hill EAST with whom I have had contact as teacher and advisor. They have shown me that our world will survive and that they will lead us all into the 21st century with a positive attitude and with hard work, as they strive to achieve world peace and cultural understanding.

Special Acknowledgments	*ix*
Introduction	*xi*
Forward	*xiii*

Part One
The Anticipation of, the Preparation for, and the Speculation about <u>The Future</u>

Liferace	3
The Road of Life	3
The Present	4
A College Student's Dream	5
Show Me	6
Wondering	7
Searching	8
The Choice	10
Rainbow Dreams	11
The Progress of Man?	12
Determination	12
The Mystery of Love	14
The Music of Love	15
Baldness Solution	16
Toupee or No Toupee	18
An Irritating Love Story	19
Aging Love	20

Part Two
The Observation of, the Exploration of and the Participation in Career Activities: <u>The Present</u>

Education	25
September 1st	27
The Sign-In Sheet	28
Homeroom	29
A Salute to the American Flag	30
Supervisory Duties	31
Delayed Openings	32
Coordination	34
Observation Day	36
PIP Day	37

The Extra-Help Sessions	39
Grade Reporting Sheets	40
Phone Home	41
Final Exam	42
The Saturday Morning Challenge	43
The Pencil	44
A Day in the Life of a Blackboard	46
The Teacher's Daily Schedule	48
The Changing Face of Education	49
Craig, The Spanish Teacher	50
Huevos	52
Participation	54
Adopting A Child by Mail	55
PASSPORT: A Celebration of Languages and Cultures	58
ADOPT-A-GRANDPARENT: A Community Service Program	59
Thanks to the Volunteers	60

Part Three
People, Places and Things: The Preservation of Memories
<u>The Past</u>

Introduction to Part Three	65
Hands of Time	66
Changes	67
Dental Changes	68
Embers of a Dying Flame	69
The Fate of 'Lost' Ideas	70
Double-Digit Year of 1977	72
1978 Calendar Year	73
The Summer of 1980	76
1980 (In Review)	79
Magical Moments in Time	80
Frankie (A Tribute to a Receptionist)	82
An AAG Farewell Message to Jean	83
A Tribute to Mr. Richard M. Smith	85
Michael Jack Schmidt	86
The Wilted Rose	87
Paradise Postponed	88
PANCHO	90
PANCHO (A Tribute)	96
The Death of Shade and Foliage	98

Part Four
The Anticipation of, the Participation in and the Contemplation of Leisure-Time Activities... <u>From Future to Present to Past</u>

Relaxation	103
Time Rhymes	104
An Early Morning Takeoff	105
A Fantasy Vacation	106
A Day in the Life of a Spider	107
A Butterfly With a Wrinkled Wing	108
Mother Nature and the Walkman	110
Nature's Song	111
The Lake	112
The Fishermen	113
The Pelican	114
A Summer Lesson in Life	115
The Water Hazard	116
Vacation - Bound	118
Model Towns	120
Sunset from Above the Clouds	121
Strangers and Friends	123
The Road With No Name	124
The Silent Silo	125
A Day at Lawrence Welk Villas	126
BINGO	127
"Ah One and Ah Two and Ah..."	128
A Different Way of Life	129
Joys of Early Morning	130
Sugarcane Rain	131
Maui Movements	136
Evening in Paradise	137
The Solar Eclipse of 1991	138
Beachfront Dining	140
Jesse Nakooka	142
Hawaiian Sky Drama	144
MAUI	145
A Fleeting Glimpse of Paradise	146
"Afterword"	148

Special Acknowledgments

I wish to recognize several individuals who have contributed a great deal to my personal development ... as an educator and as a human being. Without their contributions, my life would have been very different indeed! Special thanks are extended to:

Ruth E. Burgess, my mother, whose patience and support have resulted in my success in what I have chosen to do, both in the classroom and in the community.

Miss Bertha Dornbach (deceased), whose work-ethic in teaching Math at Audubon High School provided me with a solid background in problem-solving that has proven invaluable in every aspect of my adult life.

Mr. Richard M. Smith, Music Director at Audubon High School, whose enthusiasm for music sparked an interest in me and motivated me to continue participating in musical activities after graduating from AHS — a participation that continues today.

Mr. Fred Belchikoff, the Activities Coordinator at Cherry Hill High School EAST, whose untiring efforts in encouraging the participation of students in EAST's many extra-curricular activities have provided us all with a genuine role-model for hard work, responsibility and school spirit.

Mr. Ben Accardi, Head Administrator of the MERIDIAN HEALTHCARE CENTER in Voorhees, New Jersey, whose support and understanding have contributed greatly to the success of the Adopt-A-Grandparent program at EAST .... AND ....

Mrs. Amy Maricondi, the Director of Therapeutic Recreation at MERIDIAN, whose enthusiasm and lively personality have made the Adopt-A-Grandparent program at EAST a meaningful community service project for all of the student members.

Mr. Robert Yellen, the photographer for the EAST Yearbook, whose professionalism and sense of humor have resulted in some fantastic visual images of EAST which will live forever in our memories. (Mr. Yellen took the photograph of me doffing my Lawrence Welk Villa cap near the Main Entrance of the school that appears on the last page of this collection of poems.)

Introduction

The following collection of poems represents my feelings and impressions of life during the last half of the 20th century. It presents elements of the ANTICIPATION of, the PREPARATION for, the OBSERVATION and EXPLORATION of, the INSPIRATION and EXHILARATION resulting from and some SPECULATION concerning possible outcomes of the world in which we live and the activities which influence our daily lives.

The selections in this collection cover a period of more than 25 years and include a wide variety of points of view: from a sad, pessimistic outlook of to a happy, fun-loving glimpse of those experiences which help to shape our individual personalities.

In some of the selections, the situations are personalized in order to convey a specific feeling or emotion that I have experienced, while in others the emphasis is on a more universal view of the situation.

I have included some prose interludes because I want you, the reader, to become an active participant in the poetic adventures, rather than merely a passive reader of a collection of poems. The prose interludes offer some insight into the experiences which contribute to the development of a lifestyle.

One of many photographic memories of an exciting 30-day tour of Central and South America in 1975, this photo helps me recall my trip to the lost city of the Incas, Machu Picchu. The animals in the photo are the alpaca and the llama. Both are common to the high elevations in the Andes Mountains in Peru.

Foreword

There once was a writer of poems
Who expressed his reflections on life.
He liked what he did
And no secrets he hid
As he talked about peace and of strife.

There once was a reader of poems
Who was searching for something unique
To make him feel well
And perhaps even tell
How in life some success one could seek.

There once was a small book of poems
That was placed on a small bookstore's shelf.
It silently sat...
Like some young diplomat
Who might soon make a name for himself.

There once was a happy reunion
Of that reader in search of some clues
With verses sincere
That, in words nice and clear,
Chased away all his troublesome blues.

There once was a writer of poems
Who made readers view Life with content...
'Tho he never knew
That some dreams had come true
Thanks to thoughts which in poems he'd sent.

Any adventure in life begins with preparation, continues with investigation and observation of what is experienced, results in jubilation, exhilaration and, yes, some contemplation and speculation of the experiences, and ends with a presentation of the experiences to others. As an educator, traveler and poet, I shall begin my adventures with...

A Travelling Poet's Prelude

When a traveler is packing, preparing to leave
For some new and exciting locale,
It seems as though Time is a trustworthy friend:
Indeed, one could say, it's his pal.

When a traveler starts traveling, to widen his views
Of his world and the shape it is in,
He may quickly discover that what he has done
Is confuse what now is and what's been!

When a traveler is traveling, through Space and through Time,
To reach some enchanting new site,
His past seems to fade into billows of mist...
Just as day disappears into night.

When a traveler has landed on some distant shore
And discovers his sought after dream,
He quickly forgets all the plans that were made...
Which now, How remote they do seem!

When a traveler returns to the place he had left
In his quest to discover the world,
He finds he's a stranger in his own stomping grounds,
For in NEW set routines he's been hurled.
When a poet starts writing of what he has done
In his travels through Time and through Space,
He enables the reader to travel along

And be present in each new found place.
The effect on the reader of the poet's short trips--
From one sought after dream to the next
Is that he'll want to travel, as soon as he can,
To relive what he's read in the text!

As a poet and traveler, who's seen quite a lot
On the highways and byways of Life,
I challenge YOU, reader, to pack up your bags:
Go in search of those dreams in YOUR Life!!

Part One
The Anticipation of, the Preparation for and the Speculation about

The Future

What a way to encourage participation in Life! As we set off into the unknown to experience the wonders of the world that surrounds us, we should pause for a moment to think about Man's...

Liferace

Ever-striving,
Never done.....
That is how
Man's Life is run!

As we strive to do our best in all that we attempt, we must keep in mind that, in spite of an organized effort to prepare well for each new situation, there will be many unanticipated 'surprises' that will be encountered along...

The Road of Life

Life is quite a complex road,
With twists and curves and bends.
It offers many scenic views
Of beauty without end.
But most of us will never know
What scenic views exist:
We're always concentrating
On the next expected twist!
So, as we travel down life's road,
The views are passed unseen...
And thus we rarely get to know
What LIVING really means.

From the moment when we set forth on our first voyage of discovery (as Christopher Columbus did in that historic year of 1492), we are faced with an ongoing struggle with TIME. How long will it take to arrive at the next destination? How long should we remain there? How will we know when it is time to leave? We plan for the Future, live in the Present and reminisce about the Past. The most important of the three - - and the one which is most often neglected - is...

The Present

Oh anticipated Present,
How eagerly I await you
As you awake and stealthily creep
Into my world of schemes.

    Oh deceptive Present,
    How suddenly you appear...
    Before giving any warning
    As to just how long you'll last.

Oh nonexistent Present
On which so much depends...
Turning dreams into longed-for memories,
Leaving the searcher quite aghast.

Oh fickle Present,
How unwilling to remain...
Briefly looked for in the Future,
Then forever lost in the Past.

    Oh bygone Present,
    How swiftly I watch you set
    Into that vast sea of memories,
    Beyond a horizon of unfulfilled dreams.

But how can we make our dreams become reality BEFORE they turn into mere memories of what might have been? What can we do to insure success in our daily lives?

As I began to reminisce about my youth, I came across a delightful little poem that I had written at the beginning of my Senior year at Rutgers University, in October of 1966. I had just turned 22 and, for a few moments, had turned my thoughts to a topic which is common to all college Seniors of every generation...

A College Student's Dream

One day I met a college boy
Whose days were always filled with joy.
He was as happy as could be,
And this is what he said to me:

"My life is filled with ecstasy!
My joy lies in activity!
And when I graduate next year,
My future plans are very clear:
I want to help my fellow men
With much hard work-not with a pen!

And there's a sweet girl in my life
Who, someday soon, will be my wife.
I'll soon be teaching in a school
Where students learn THE GOLDEN RULE.
My wife, a mother soon will be,
And our lives filled with-joy will be.
We'll take an interest in our land
And, against our enemies, take a stand...
For we'll find love and great reward
In being able to help the Lord."

Now, when that student left my side,
I felt as if I could have cried.
If each of us could feel as he,
What a great future there would be!

But, can't you see, I'm not so smart,
I should have known this from the start:
Our youth today IS filled with hope,
And with future problems will ably cope.
Thus all of us should feel so proud
That we could shout the words aloud:

"Our world to greatness still can climb!
The only thing we need is TIME!!!"

Those thoughts were quite optimistic for the late 1960's. When I graduated from Rutgers in 1967, Joan Baez was one of the more popular folk singers. One of her songs-- one which fascinated me-was entitled *There but for Fortune*. I wrote my own set of lyrics to accompany the melody of this intriguing folk song. My mind, caught in a web of conflicting and confusing concepts, from war to racial discrimination to signs of desperation which had begun to appear throughout the nation, began to envision the influence of the Present on the society of the Future. I found myself reaching out and providing some outcomes to all of those situations which society had been attempting to...

Show Me

Show me the people who peace were praying for.
Show me the government that tried to conquer war.
And I'll show you a graveyard, with coffins by the score,
Since only with the death of Man can there be an end to war.

Show me a college grad, just waiting for success.
Show me a married girl in a newly purchased dress.
And I'll show you a nation where no one really cares
If tomorrow may bring happiness, or only more despairs.

But show me a student who tries to aid the poor,
Or show me a scientist who sickness does explore...
And I'll show you the future of the world which we have made:
A future filled with all those things for which Mankind has prayed.

Please show me a fruit tree with all its fruit in bloom,
Or show me a great big house with kids who fill each room...
And I'll show you the greatest sight that human eyes can see:
The future of our prosperous land and, of course, of YOU AND ME.

As all of us mature and begin investigating and exploring the world around us, we find ourselves experiencing situations which are at times positive in nature and at times negative. I had a very positive outlook for the future as I graduated from college, but there were times when I found myself...

Wondering

The furry gloves
The cooing doves
The songs of love
The stars above...
And WONDERING.

Can we be sure
That faith is pure?
Or perfect the cure
That we secure
With WONDERING?

And what remains
Of all the plains? . .
And all men's pains
For wealth and gains?...
But WONDERING!

We shout and holler
About the dollar.
But am I taller
By being a scholar?
I'm WONDERING...

We'll never know
What makes the glow
Of glistening snow
On someone's toe
By WONDERING!

Can we exist
And not resist
The fateful fist
Of atomic mist?
I'm WONDERING!

My friends, struggle not!
For I've been taught
That we're ALL caught
In the embers hot
Of WONDERING!

And when MY life's through,
There'll still be YOU!...
And who but you
Can begin anew
MY WONDERING?

Oh, the complexity of mental activity! And the more we contemplate our surroundings, the more we envision images of destruction, construction, instruction and production-which play a role in our existence. As a result, we are constantly...

Searching

We write and we scribble
While basketballs dribble
And, as for replies,
Hear only the cries
Of the infants who simper
And hound dogs that whimper-
Without any knowledge
Of high school or college
As they search for a future,
And for some timely suture
Which might bring an end
To a most deadly trend:
DESTRUCTION!

But can it be found,
In a crib or the pound,
This long sought device?...
For ending the strife
And leading us on,
With brain and not brawn,
To an age of success

That places all stress
On the solid foundation
Of securing a nation
Linked together by faith
Which unites every race
In the glorious fight
To achieve that great sight:
    CONSTRUCTION!

For the gigantic task...
Of discarding the mask
That covers the world
So that, once it's unfurled,
The flag of Peace
May bring a cease
To all this Destruction
Which produced a reduction
In the marvels of Man
And, flying high, can -
In an age sound and sure-
Establish the cure
Which eliminates strife
And perpetuates life:
    INSTRUCTION!...

Can only be done
When we look to the sun
And place our devotion,
Not in some potion
But, ...in our Creator
Who, as an Orator,
Has given us hope -
For increasing the scope
Of this world of ours -
By expanding our powers ...
Through increased education
And reduced segregation...
By employing as guide
That which gives us much pride:
PRODUCTION!

Yes! *Production!... The* result of our planning. Let's hope that our planning has been successful so that we will be prepared to face the future and find happiness when it comes time to make...

The Choice

There comes a time in everyone's life
When he must choose between peace and strife.
And when that moment comes for me,
I think I know what my choice will be.

In a world that's filled with tension and hate,
Man finds it difficult to watch and wait.
He feels he must support some cause
In a valiant effort to preserve the laws.
But does he believe that he is right
If he creates more tension by his might?...
Or is it that he doesn't see
What the results of his actions could be??

I'm not a man who tries to pretend
That the importance of acting is the longed-for end,
For I cannot dedicate my entire self
To working for a trophy to place on a shelf.

I hope that when all of us make 'the choice',
It will be with some action, not just with our voice...
For the future awaiting the 'now' generation
Depends on much more than vocalization.

Our parents have witnessed the changes vast
Which upon the world OUR age has cast.
And, at times, they seem a bit concerned
About the goals to which our sights have been turned.

The future of our world rests in our hands.
It involves-all peoples; it involves all lands.
Think about this BEFORE you decide.....
For AFTER you have chosen, there's no place to hide!!

Each of us will be faced with many moments of doubt and uncertainty as we challenge the unknown and work to improve our society. I would compare these moments of doubt to a cloudy, rainy day which, as clearing occurs, provides some views of

Rainbow Dreams

The clouds were as dark as a tunnel,
And appeared to be frowning in pain,
As their tears flowed, unending, upon me
(What everyone else knows as rain).
As I slowly walked on through the darkness,
My vision still blurred by those 'tears',
It seemed as though Life held no meaning
As days quickly turned into years.

But then, a promising thing happened:
Those teardrops were ceasing to fall.
And the clouds were changing in color
As through them the sun came to call.

I felt that my 'darkness' was ending,
Burned away by the sun's warming light.
So I searched through the skies for a rainbow-
There it was! What a beautiful sight!!
As I stared at the numerous colors-
Purple, orange, green, yellow and blue-
I rejoiced, for my future seemed brighter...
And my dreams might indeed all come true!

Just as the sun's rays manage to pierce the darkness of the clouds, a positive attitude can help us pierce the darkness of those days of doubt and uncertainty... and help us in the pursuit of our dreams. These dreams may often seem 'unreachable' (as a modern Don Quixote might say), but they are NEVER impossible to achieve. Our constant search for improvement in every aspect of daily life is what leads to successful production in society.

Yet, as we continue to open new pathways along the road of life, we often find ourselves being bombarded with facts which, at times, seem meaningless to the achievement of those dreams. After all, how can we be certain that all of our production will result in...

The Progress of Man

Who was the man who discovered the lamp?
Who pitched the first baseball? Who licked the first stamp?
These questions at first may seem quite without sense-
Like a car without headlights or a picket-less fence.
Yet each of us knows that we live in a time
When these meaningless questions gain reason and rhyme.
For what is so great as a boy of fifteen
Who has butchered his mother like some ugly fiend?!

The age that we live in (at least so I'm told)
May never reach greatness; may never grow old,
For the bombs that we're using in striving for Peace
Will lead to destruction before they will cease.

And what can WE do, oh Men of Today?
Can we stop this destruction and reverse our decay?
That's only a question the Future can tell:
If the world rose to greatness, or to nothingness fell!

Those lines were written in 1966! And yet, with all of the trivia games being sold in today's society -- and with all of the headlines describing the brutality that occurs every day -- those lines seem to be describing the world of 1992! Indeed, while some things change, some things stay the same from generation to generation. And we DO continue to show progress, in spite of the negative influences. How?? By maintaining a positive outlook and by setting productive goals! Of course, the key to this productivity is...

Determination

What is the destination
Of our life upon the Earth?
Does it end within the graveyard?-
And, if so, what is Life's worth?
There are many pressing questions
That arise within our mind:

As to what the Future really holds
And the life that we may find.....

When a student enters college
To become a learned man,
He discovers what he cannot do-
And also what he can!
Yet many times the plans he makes
Force him to realize
That Life contains quite a number
Of problems, huge in size.
And when, at graduation,
He obtains his earned degree,
He may feel just like an animal
Trapped up in a tree.
For the vision of his future life,
Envisioned as a child,
Has changed from something wonderful
To something strange and wild!
And yet he finds he cannot quit
The struggle he began.
And so he tries, as all men try,
To achieve whate'er he can!
And when his life has ended,
And he enters into Death,
He can pride himself on all his gains
As he breathes his final breath.
What is the destination
Of our life upon the Earth?
Is it something that we learn about?
Is it inherited at birth?

I can't provide an answer
To a question of such weight,
Though I know that for each person
There exists a certain fate.
Yet I CAN give you a little hint
That will aid you in your quest:
You must have DETERMINATION!
THAT will win for you each test!

In this last poem (again written in 1966) I mentioned the influence of those problems with which we are faced in our daily lives. One of the most exhilarating -- and frustrating -- problems which we encounter is known as LOVE. Everyone's life is influenced in one or more ways by this enigmatic facet of life. That influence may be spiritual, it may be physical, or it may even be platonic, but one thing is certain: it is VERY difficult to comprehend ...

The Mystery of Love

LOVE is such a wondrous thing!
It's mentioned everyday
In every clime and culture
From Spain to Prudhoe Bay.
But few can really comprehend
What LOVE is all about...
That mixture of emotions
Which makes one cheer OR pout!
For LOVE has no reality
That anyone can see.
It penetrates beyond our sight
To set our spirit free.
And each of us approaches LOVE
In such a different way:
For LOVE is based on lifestyle
And on how we live each day.
So when YOU reach that goal in life
Which fills your soul with LOVE,
Be thankful that your journey
Has been guided from Above!

Spiritual love plays an important role in most of our lives. The heavenly nature of it provides joy and jubilation. I often look upon LOVE in the same way that I look at the words of a song, because the words and the musical accompaniment in a song do not always represent the entire meaning. There is often something more which is intangible; something which may be reflected in...

The Music of Love

We know writers compose all the lyrics
For composers who write all the songs
But, though they be sweet,
All those words can't compete
With the feelings to which love belongs...
For the lyrics are seen only on paper
And the melodies heard only when played,
But love's TRUE harmonies
Don't need ink, don't need keys-
Just two people's real feelings displayed.
So don't let your mind wander through lyrics!
Don't let your ears search for the tune!
For the music of Love
Has been sent from Above
On the light of the stars and the moon.
Keep in mind that sweet words are deceptive
And that tunes quickly fade from our ears,
While the light from Above
Plays the music of love
On the heartstrings of lovers for years.

How fickle the world of Love! And how often we are misled by appearances! As a recent college grad and a new teacher, I was faced with an interesting predicament: I was only 22 years old, but I was almost completely BALD! What a sad state of affairs! My mental powers and enthusiasm reflected my youth, while my physical appearance reflected "retirement". What could I do? What should I do? AHA!! I will solve my problem..... AND surprise all of my "friends and colleagues".......... with a TOUPEE! What a great...

Baldness Solution!

Who, disguised as that Sporty youth,
Was that young man in the telephone booth?
'Twas that young Spanish prof named Craig...
Whose balding scalp resembled an egg
Before that bright and sunny day
When late October turned to May!

Return with us now to yesteryear,
So far away and yet so near,
And learn the secret of this lad...
And the great adventure that he had!

It was a sunny August morn
On which he found himself reborn.
The building into which he went
Helped create for him a new 'Clark Kent':
By eliminating those shades of bare
And providing him with much more hair!
The transformation which he could see
Produced overwhelming alegrity,
For the aging image he had seen
Had now become that of a youthful teen!

And when he returned that fateful morn,
His newly fitted hairpiece worn,
His neighbor couldn't believe his eyes
When he perceived Craig in his new guise!
And several persons let him know
That it was good he let his hair <u>grow</u>!

And so, my friends, you see: IT'S TRUE!
The man in the phone booth could be YOU!
It doesn't take a lot of bread
To make a rich meadow from a deserted head!
It only takes a sense of pride...
And a sense of humor on the side!!!

Of course, it also required a little 'intestinal fortitude' to be able to walk into a classroom filled with students who had already seen the 'natural look'. I adjusted well, but I soon began to wonder what had really prompted me to seek such a 'coverup' as a solution. After all, was the new 'image' worth the time spent each morning trying to secure the hairpiece? Had I indeed become a better person because of the change in physical appearance? Of course not! And so it was that, with increased self-confidence in my daily teaching responsibilities AND in my ability to achieve success and happiness WITHOUT a disguise, the time came for a second important decision in my social life: do away with the hairpiece!

As I now reflect on that BIG MOMENT in my life, I realize that physical appearance is not everything (even though it does help). And I could not help but bring to mind that famous passage of William Shakespeare entitled TO BE OR NOT TO BE. I read over the lines of the passage several times and then decided to take on an interesting challenge: that of writing a poem in the Shakespeare-style which would describe that moment in time when I made the decision to remove the disguise and display with pride my balding pate. But... what would I call such a piece of poetry? Could there be any doubt about the title? It was a natural (no pun intended). I would entitle such a work .....

Toupee or No Toupee

Toupee, or NO toupee: That was the question.
Whether 'twoud be better for my self-image
To wear the matted hair and plastic meshing,
Or go with balding pate into the classroom
And just ignore the laughter; to tape or tape
No more; and by to tape I mean to place
The hairpiece and then rearrange the placement,
Caress the hairless dome. What test of patience!
And all for what? To hold in place for hours,
To hold? Perchance entwine! Yes, that's what hurts,
For when it's held secure, there's also pain
When next it is removed from tender skin,
Which then glows red: the end result
Of such repeated morning acts of care;
For he who tapes and pulls the lifeless hair
Must grin and bear it, to handsomely appear
When out in public be amongst the crowds
Of would-be scorners, and ignore, to boot,
The often whispered jokes of his jealous friends,
When he himself might also jealous be
Of those with more hair, and would, thus, conceal,
In hope of making some great impression,
That balding pate which is itself, indeed,
A symbol of much great activity,
For thus, no hair returns to cover up
What God has chosen as a special shape,
Developed from so many sleepless nights.
The hairpiece would make cowards of those few
Who have chosen to conceal, and not display,
What so many only hope for in their dreams.
And so it seemed, after two long years of tape,
That better things might well accomplished be
If I remained toupee-less.

Please forgive me, Mr. Shakespeare. It's just that I found that I could not resist the challenge. But, getting back to reality, was my life now to be deprived of 'true love' since I had no hair? Since I am still a bachelor, my decision must have had some influence on romance. Perhaps, perhaps not. I can tell you that for many years I was being pursued... AND that being bald meant absolutely nothing in the 'romance'. Unfortunately, these romantic encounters proved to be nothing more than .....

An Irritating Love Story

My love affair with Ivy
I still can't understand,
And though I've tried to stay away,
She reaches for my hand
Whenever I am unaware
That she is lurking near...
And so I break out in a rash
Which takes much time to clear!

Oh, Ivy, you're so delicate,
So illusive and so vain:
Advancing, disappearing,
Then coming back again!
You hide among the bushes,
Just blowing in the wind,
Until, when least expected,
You creep beneath my skin!
If only I could stay away
Whenever you advance,
My arms would never itch again...
The result of our "romance!"

Oh, Ivy, can't you understand
That we can NOT be wed!
For you are just like poison
(Or so I've heard it said).
And ev'ryone who's met you
Knows you really are quite wily...
You STEM-FATALE with shiny leaves,
Well-known as POISON IVY !!!

Ah! ROMANCE!! But... what is this thing called ROMANCE?? It leads us to do strange deeds and often keeps us awake at night. But how long will it really last? And what will result from our efforts to fulfill those dreams associated with ROMANCE?? For while many of us live happily everafter, with the 'music of love' playing in our souls, there are those who plan strategies that prove unsuccessful and who then are faced with a different outcome: that of

Aging Love

Like a shadow in a shade tree
My love awaits its chance:
The coming of a partner
With whom it soon will dance,
Enveloping with youthful joy --
As the oyster does its pearl --
A sweetly-scented bosom,
Caressing some sweet girl.

Yet, just as shade trees wither,
Thus losing all their shade,
My passion now has withered
While awaiting that fair maid.
And so I see no int'rest
In searching far and wide
Since, like the withered shade tree,
My longing now has died.
And all that's left are mem'ries
Of shadows long since gone...
Oh, Love, what now awaits me
As life continues on??

What a unique way to summarize the first part of my poetic presentation: the eager anticipation of success and happiness, the preparation for expected events, and some speculation about the possible outcomes of both.

Let's now turn our attention to what goes on in daily life. As an educator, I am anxious to acquaint you, the reader, with some of the joys AND disappointments associated with the teaching profession.

As we enter the second part of my journey, please keep in mind that for ME teaching has been my 'true' Love. While ROMANCE quite often is temporary and fleeting, LOVE is something that remains and becomes stronger with age. My LOVE for teaching has done just that!

Part Two

**The Observation of,
the Exploration of
and the Participation in
Career Activities:**

The Present

As I begin the second part of my journey - my career as an educator - I will present an overview of

Education

Memorization
    The skill developed through study,
    In specific structured patterns,
    Of names, dates and accomplishments,
    Relating History to Culture.

Repetition
    The activity for thought acquisition,
    Through aural and visual approaches,
    Designed to establish brain patterns
    For investigating trends in society.

Integration
    A process of combining the structures,
    Repeated and properly memorized,
    Into new and exciting expressions
    Which relate to historical and cultural trends.

Proficiency
    The ability to perform in society
    With knowledge of new structures
    And evidence of great self-assurance,
    Using those integrated structures.

On paper, these four processes would seem to lead us all to the development of the "perfect" student and citizen. However, there are two negatives which have a habit of creeping into the situation (just as Ivy will 'creep beneath your skin') :

Frustration
> The result of that process quite useless:
> The attempt being made by the <u>"learned"</u>
> To accomplish the proficiency goals
> Without developing the required brain patterns.

Deprivation
> The current sad state of our populace
> Which resulted from futile attempts
> To develop the brain by hand-power
> And computerization of knowledge!...
> For when the electrical current
> Causes memory failure in chips,
> The hand-power learning is useless
> And the HUMAN brain can not respond.

The four important processes in education have as their objective the development of a well-rounded individual. With new advances in technology being integrated into the educational setting each year, the educator finds that he or she is both teacher and learner as each new school year begins. Many interesting (and often frustrating) situations arise as the educator works in the classroom, trying to satisfy the needs of the students as they seek knowledge and understanding AND the needs of the school administration as it seeks excellence in performance and achievement. As a result, the teacher anticipates the excitement of the classroom and reminisces about those fleeting weeks of summer break every year on...

September 1st

Great days of summer
Filled with fun and excitement-
Visions of the past.

New groups of students,
Eager to pursue learning,
Soon will come to class.

Profs on vacation,
Resting from the past year's work,
Plan the first day's speech.

Pigskins replace gloves
As baseball yields to football
On fields everywhere.

And I reminisce
On how I spent MY summer
At home and away.

How quickly they've gone:
June, July and August...
Another summer.

Now it's time for you to follow in my footsteps as I provide you with some of the daily experiences associated with the teaching profession. Since all of you are quite familiar with the normal routines in the classroom (having experienced them first-hand), I shall emphasize some of the activities and responsibilities with which you may not be so familiar. Let's begin with some thoughts about the early morning activities and duties of each teacher, whose day begins when he or she approaches ...

The Sign-In Sheet

I get to school at 6:45
From September until June.
I like to come in early...
And leave late each afternoon.
My first responsibility
Is to go up to a wall
And sign a sheet of paper-
It's a silent-type ROLL CALL!
By checking out this sign-in sheet,
You get to know the staff...
By how they 'note' their presence-
It can sometimes make one laugh!
Some sign a different way each day,
Some use a different ink,
And some don't bother signing in,
Thus showing what THEY think!

The teachers proceed to their classes, where they prepare themselves for the first activity of the school day:

Homeroom

Each morning at just about 7:45
A bell resounds all through the school:
A signal for students to quicken their pace
To avoid that incredible duel
That occurs in the office at about 8:05...
Because lateness occurred once again,
By failing to get to HOMEROOM on time! -
What will happen today by 8:10?

Like cattle in chutes they must run through the halls
While the teachers keep prodding them on:
"Just TWO minutes more, then the late bell will ring.
Get moving! Don't just stand there and yawn!"

The late bell announces, at 8:00 am sharp,
That HOMEROOM again has begun.
You should be in your room and be perfectly still
So all the teacher's work can be done:
There's attendance to check on and notes to be read,
And even some passes to give
For Guidance appointments or meetings with staff.
(Does the Principal ever forgive?)
There are forms to complete of every type-
From the school or, perhaps, from the State-
And all must be finished by at least 8:08.
Gee, HOMEROOM is definitely great!!

What a nice and relaxing way to start the day!!? (And some of you were thinking ONLY about the class presentations for which the teacher must prepare... How soon 'we' forget!)

I can not leave Homeroom without including a personal thought related to an important activity that occurs each morning at 8:01. At that time each day, everyone is asked to stand for the FLAG SALUTE. For all of us this moment should be (although sometimes it doesn't seem to be) a time to show pride in that great symbol of our nation. I feel fortunate that I have the opportunity each day to take a moment to give...

A Salute to the American Flag

Each time I see my country's flag
Unfurled and hanging high,...
Caressed by gentle breezes
To wave as I go by;
Displaying all those mighty stripes
Of vibrant red and white;
Accompanied by brilliant stars
Indeed an awesome sight! ...
It brings to mind the pride I feel
For what my nation's done:
Those marvelous accomplishments
Which make our nation one!

Great symbol of our Promised Land
In bright red, white and blue:
Forever wave in majesty
For all of us to view!!

Following Homeroom, each teacher has a schedule made up of at least five classes, with two or three different preparations. In addition, there are some additional exciting responsibilities known as...

Supervisory Duties

In addition to TEACHING each day of the year,
With FIVE classes and THREE lesson plans
We each are assigned
(And we really don't mind!)
To a series of additional and required demands.

The most likely assignment is a Homeroom each day,
With attendance sheets we must complete.
And with it will fall
A large Study Hall
In which students are given a pre-assigned seat.
For those who dislike all THESE daily routines,
With attendance and announcements galore,
An alternative neat
Is that of a seat
Supervising the students - with 3 colleagues or more-
Who have come to the school Cafeteria lines
To select from the menu some good things to eat.
You must keep them INSIDE,
And you do it with PRIDE!
But Stay Out of the Lunchroom if You Can't Stand the Heat!

And speaking of "daily routines," what happens when the routines are interrupted unexpectedly? Why, flexibility comes into play! Take, for instance, this view of the impact on planning caused by...

Delayed Openings

'Twas the eve of the twelfth of December
As I 'plotted my course' for the week:
With a test to be given on Tuesday-
With some special vocab words to seek
In a section entitled "Repaso"-
With the goal of reviewing the book
From the first seven units of grammar
And a story of three cops and a crook.

The review had been set for the fourteenth,
With the test on the following day.
All went well in that Monday review class,
But on Tuesday, the plans went astray...
For late Monday the clouds they did thicken
And the temperature started to fall
So by midnight it was well below freezing
And some snowflakes had started to fall.
By daylight the roads were like ice rinks
And the snowplows had not yet begun
To salt and to sand all the highways...
So driving would NOT be much fun!

When my phone rang at 5:47,
I knew who the caller would be:
A colleague who'd give me a message,
"LATE OPENING" -- Oh, how could that be!!
The exam was my finest one ever
And would challenge my classes, no doubt.
But each class would be twelve minutes shorter!
What test items could be left out???

I answered the phone and said: "Thank you,",
Then called assigned friends on the sheet.
And, after some moments of worry,
Decided what parts to delete
On this marvelous evaluation
Of the progress of each of my kids...
I'd cut out the two compositions-
Of much marking time it thus rids!

Oh, woe is the classroom instructor
Who plans all his days in advance,
Quite forgetting that old "Mother Nature"
Is the victor, when given the chance.

Speaking of woes, another aspect of teaching that can become rather aggravating is that which deals with the preparation of materials for class AND the pace at which these materials are introduced, practiced, reviewed and evaluated during the course of the school year. It is well known as...

Coordination

I love teaching Spanish.
It makes me feel great!
But one aspect of teaching
I HAVE learned to hate.
It could be called planning,
But whatever its name,
It drives teachers crazy-
And that's really a shame!!
When assignments are given
For sections to teach,
There are two or more colleagues
As instructors for each.
Each one has his methods
For presenting the facts;
Thus, when put together,
The results are ATTACKS!

   *   "I want to test Tuesday."
  **   "I won't be prepared."
   *   "Then I must report you."
  **   "But I thought you cared."
***   "We MUST stay together
      And finish the text."
  **   "I can't teach that quickly
      One week to the next!"
***   "You need some assistance
      To learn what to skip."

** "You need to teach students
At a moderate clip."
 * "You shouldn't be teaching
At level III A."
** "I know what I'm doing!
Let's do it MY way!"

So, week after week,
The discussions go on,
With no one agreeing
Before each month's gone.
But after each unit,
When testing is done,
The students have shown
That the job can be fun.
And though there are diff'rences
In classroom approach,
At the end of the school year
Each has been a fine coach!

If only instruction
Were designed for results,
Instead of by Chairmen-
Teamed up into cults -
Who try to confuse us
By hook or by crook
As we plan each day's lessons
With the help of the book.

"We've been teaching for decades!
Good results have been shown!
We know what we're doing-
So LEAVE US ALONE!!!"

Can't you just feel the exhilaration associated with teaching. I bet a lot of you are now wishing that you had become teachers! But.... wait a minute. Let me tell you a little more about the role of the "Chairperson" in the lives of teachers. One event that ALL teachers look forward to (!?) is that evaluation of ability which occurs on...

Observation Day

I'd prepared my lesson fairly well
(Or at least I thought I had)
And, as I walked toward my room,
I wasn't feeling sad.
But as I entered, to begin
The lesson I had planned,
I saw the dreaded CHAIRPERSON
Seated calm!, pen in hand.
She had a copy of my plans
(Which I had made last week),
But what I was about to teach
Would make my future bleak.
For there was nothing in those plans
That matched my lesson's goals...
And so, when I would meet with her,
She'd rake me o'er the coals.
But I knew how to win the day-
And also save my job!-
I taught the class with confidence
And called on Jill and Bob...
For they were my best students:
They performed just flawlessly!
So when I got my graded sheet,
She'd given me a C !!

I should point out here that I served as a Chairperson for some six years, so I know 'from where the coals come'. My poem makes reference to a female Chairperson because it is only fair to recognize the role of women in all aspects of education.

Following the observation (or series of observations), each teacher must meet with the Chairperson and plan activities for the coming year. These activities represent a Personal Improvement Plan that is designed to keep the teacher up to date with recent developments in the field of education. The discussion session is the culmination of the evaluation process and can be described quite simply as...

PIP Day

My class observation is over
And now I must prove what I've done,
For tomorrow I meet with the chairman
To discuss how the lesson was run.
Did I know what I hoped to accomplish?
Did I know what success I achieved?
Did I base classroom drills on objectives,
Or only on things I believed?

I will have to just sit down and listen
As the chairman explains how I taught.
What a strange way to motivate colleagues
To improve on techniques being sought!

But the best part of ev'ry discussion
Involves what is called P.I.P.:
The plan for one's personal improvement...
Like a thesis for one's Ph.D.
I must think of some logical topic
To reflect upon during the year
And present before next year's discussion
In a format quite neat and quite clear.

Now.. should I investigate concepts
That the students can not comprehend?
Or make a determined commitment
To say nothing that perhaps would offend?
I don't want the chairman to dictate
The topic which I must address,
For such lack of interest on my part
Will surely result in distress.
So I'll spend the night weighing my options
And selecting what I think is best-
Then hope that the chairman misplaces
The notes which contained my request!

A toast to the great P.I.P. day
Which has given us something to do
While relaxing alone at the poolside
In the summer when skies are all blue.
It's the incentive that keeps teachers teaching!
It's what motivates us to succeed!
If only it weren't such a big waste of time,
But something we truly did need!

By now you are probably wondering why I previously stated that teaching was my 'true love'. The previous six 'scenes' would appear to represent much more frustration than exhilaration. I have discussed only one side of the educational scene up to now: the interaction between the teacher and the administration. Let's now look into the interaction of the teacher with the students and the parents. There are several fascinating aspects to this interaction (although quite often students do not take full advantage of the opportunities being made available). One example of this is the failure to remain after classes for...

The Extra Help Sessions

As each school year began in September
(In those years BEFORE classes year-round)
Each instructor was asked to comply with
A request, telling where he'd be found...
So that students in need of assistance
Would know where EXTRA HELP could be sought
As through ten months of classroom instruction
They attempted to use all that's taught.

The idea of helping the students
After class is a fine one indeed.
What is puzzling to so many teachers
Is why students this service don't heed!
For many prefer to pay tutors
(Who charge an incredible fee)
To obtain extra practice with concepts
Which are offered in school-AND for free!!

It seems useless to make out a schedule
To be followed with no change in days,
When such schedules serve no major purpose...
Since it's surprising when some student stays!
I suppose that the only real meaning
In stating such extra-help days
Is for some compilation of duties
Oft' included in School Board displays
As a way of providing the parents
With insight on daily routines.
How sad that most all of the figures
Mean nothing to parents and teens!

Unfortunately, it is often difficult to communicate concerns to parents in a personal way. Technology in the field of education has produced changes in the grade reporting process. The personal touch has, in many schools, been replaced by computerized...

Grade Reporting Sheets

Once there were teachers in schools just like mine
Who gave grades to each lad and each lass:
They hand-wrote each one
And, when comments were done,
Returned the filled cards to the class.

But modern procedures have developed a way
To give grades without wasting class time:
On computerized sheets
Each instructor completes
All the grades for each class... What a crime!
For there's nothing the teacher can subjectively say
About the progress each student has made.
He fills in the dots,
But no comments he jots-
The objective mere numbers to shade.

I should thank the computer for such a great gift
Which allows me to teach more in class,
But the students don't know
Why their grades ebb and flow...
For the numbers mean more than each lad and each lass.

I have found a way to keep the personal touch alive in the classroom, nevertheless. Every October I contact all of the parents of my students by phone in order to update them on classroom progress. This procedure allows me to get to know more about the individual students, and it also often proves to be a positive reinforcement. The most amazing aspect of this instructional technique is the reaction of many of the parents whenever I...

Phone Home

One of the things which I have learned
After twenty-five years in class
Is that talking to parents encourages kids
To do more than just study to pass.
When a student is doing exceptionally well,
The parents won't bother to call.
They assume that the teacher is doing the job:
They see grade sheets and that's about all.
And so when they learn that a teacher has called
To provide information on grades,
They immediately think that those grade sheets were wrong...
And their confidence rapidly fades.
Oh, what a surprise when they learn I have called
To give them some positive news!
For no one phones home when a student does WELL-
Just when there is no time to lose!

I enjoy making phone calls when the students do well
For it motivates more than I thought.
The parents feel happy, and so do the kids
Since their efforts DO mean quite a lot.
So parents, remember: when the telephone rings
And a teacher is calling from school,
Don't panic BEFORE you have heard the report...
They're exceptions to EVERY rule!

Let me include in this section of the 'travels' two references to student evaluation. As a teacher, I am always providing encouragement to students in the classroom. Their DETERMINATION in preparing for evaluations culminates in that dreaded...

Final Exam

The students have finally finished the course
And believe that they've learned quite a bit.
But now comes the true test of what has been taught...
And, for many, it causes a fit!
The students must come to the FINAL EXAM
Which will last for an hour and a half-
And show that they've mastered, from September to June,
The skills which were set by the staff.

They must think! And recall many places and names!
And, of course, demonstrate what to do
With all of the structures innate to the course...
Quite often with nary a clue!
For some, the exams are approached with a smile
And a confident outlook indeed!
While others are hoping to score enough points
To achieve that great grade that they need!
But all of the students would achieve so much more
If the FINALS were tests WITHOUT scores!
For then they could simply apply what they've learned
Without sweat streaming out of their pores!

And speaking of perspiration, a student comes face to face with one written evaluation during his or her high school years that is often approached with great trepidation: the all-encompassing SAT exam. This exam is, without a doubt, ...

The Saturday Morning Challenge

On a warm Springtime morning at 11:15
I sat quietly behind a big desk,
Watching 43 students who had come to my school
For the purpose of taking a test.
There were 35 "walk-ins" who decided to come,
And 8 others who paid in advance.
But all of them had but one goal in their minds
As into the room they did prance:
They wanted to go to an excellent school
After leaving the high school environs...
And begin once again the exciting routine-
From Science to the life of the Sirens.
But first they must take that horrendous first step
Which everyone once must attempt:
The dreaded exam called (of course) S A T
Of which they have probably dreamt.
So for three endless hours their minds madly searched
For the answers to questions unique.
And if they have finished before time is called
They may even decide just to 'peek'
At the upcoming section: with problems galore,
With more stories, or perhaps some more math.
And, Oh, how they long for that ultimate choice
That awaits at the end of the path!
It's an int'resting job watching students at work
As they fret and they sigh and they smile,
And they all seem relieved as they head for the door,
Having conquered their first lifetime trial.

What an overview! Attention has been given to the role of the chairpeople, the teachers, the students and even the parents in the educational setting. Two other very important items have not as yet been covered... AND most often are completely overlooked. I would like to give each some credit for their contributions to the educational process. I shall begin with a description - from a unique 'point' of view - of...

The Pencil

My owner purchased me today in a local 5 and 10
And took me to her study room: I knew she'd be my friend!
But then a strange thing happened. Oh, what a shock it was!
She took me to a metal case which had begun to buzz...
She held me in her fingertips and placed me near the sound:
I can't believe it's happening! MY BODY'S BEING GROUND!!
I can't believe the pain I feel as blades release my lead,
And though I'm now quite pointed... I thought that I'd be DEAD!
I know Life can be painful and that scars will oft' appear,
But WHY she was so cruel to me was really not too clear...

She took me out of that machine and gently brushed my head,
Then sat down at a table where a book was she had read.
She took a sheet of paper from the package she had bought,
And brought me to its surface-and held me, deep in thought.
She started moving me along the surface of that sheet,
And what appeared from my sharp point were thoughts so nice and neat.
My Life now has some meaning and will play a brilliant role,
For my lead will live FOREVER on some all important scroll!!

Now my friend has gone away and left me all alone.
My point has nearly disappeared; thus soon I'll once more moan
As through that metal sharpener my Skin will pass again
Until my lead is sharpened... Gee, I wish I were a PEN!

At least I can appreciate what Life is all about:
There will be times of greatness, as well as times of doubt.
Yet I have learned to persevere the loneliness and pain,
For, once I hit that paper, I produce results germane
To many dif'rent topics hidden deep in human thought...
And so it makes me happy:
        THAT'S WHY I HAD BEEN WROUGHT!!!

What a valuable instrument! The pencil serves the students well in the preparation of assignments, in the taking of tests (including the SAT) and, in general, in the expression of ideas.

The second item of great importance is that marvelous writing surface known as the blackboard (which now is green in color in many classrooms). It also is taken for granted by both students and teachers. And yet, without the blackboard, how different would be the educational setting. Come with me as I describe for you...

A Day in the Life of a Blackboard

As dawn again breaks in the clear eastern skies,
And the Sun's rays come into my room,
I savor the moment of their radiant warmth
After hours of shadow and gloom.
The effect of the cleaning on the previous eve
Left me shivering from dusk until dawn,
With streaks of caked chalk spread across my whole face-
Just the traces of facts long since gone.

As the Sun seeks its zenith and removes its warm rays,
I can hear the approach of a class
Which soon will be seated in front of my 'screen'
Taking notes from some topic en masse
As my friend, an instructor, creates, with great haste,
A great series of letters and words
Designed to increase the awareness of facts:
Of Math, perhaps Science, even birds.
Then, as a computer, the screen quickly clears
And is filled with a new set of clues...
To be used as the keys that will open the minds
Of the students who will soon spread the news.

As the day hastens onward, more students come in
And another instructor comes near...
To erase what was written and prepare something new
For HIS CLASS, as exam time draws near.
For eight separate classes old facts are erased
And a new program placed on my 'screen'
Until, when the last class has left for the day,
Once again I am washed 'til I'm clean!

I'm amazed at the knowledge that crosses my 'mind'
As I help all the students to learn
About all of the subjects so important to Life
Which those teachers display, each in turn.
And I'm proud that my surface resists wear and tear
Through the months and the years of much use. ...

If only the students could hear my lament
When they use my great 'face' for abuse!
For they never consider the role that I play
In the growth of their knowledge of facts:
They just take for granted that I'll always be there,
Just a slate for artistic attacks!

The Sun is now setting in the far western skies,
And I shiver in the dark and the gloom
As the custodian leaves and locks up the door
That gives access to my precious room.

    As you can now see, the only difference between a blackboard and a computer screen is that a blackboard does not come equipped with a memory in which to store material which has been written on its surface.... Or does it?
    Now that you have a little better idea of what goes on 'behind the scenes' in a school and in the classroom, I have a question for you: Have you written a note or sent a greeting card to your favorite teacher recently? WHAT!! You haven't?? After all that he or she has done for YOU! Shame on you!! Perhaps I can encourage you to participate in such a writing activity by summarizing...

The Teacher's Daily Schedule

His day begins at 6:00 am (before the Sun appears)
And doesn't end'til late at night, as midnight quickly nears.
Success in what he does each day depends on his approach:
On what he says and how he states set structures, like a coach.
He must enjoy the work he does in order to fulfill
The goals he's set for each new week-and meet those goals he will.
For he approaches challenges with confidence and pride,
And never gets discouraged when the targets tend to hide.
Do YOU know what this person does to earn his daily bread?
Why, of course, he was your teacher, who has helped you get ahead.
For, after graduation day from the school in which he taught,
You realized how much you'd learned --- and that was quite a lot!
Why don't you take a minute from your successful climb...
And drop him just a little note... and THANK HIM for his time!

Have I made you feel a bit "guilty"? Well, don't wait TOO long to send that little note. Remember the advice given to all of us by Harry Chapin in his song CAT'S IN THE CRADLE and by Don Williams in his recent release entitled STANDING KNEE DEEP IN A RIVER, DYING OF THIRST.

As we well know, education is changing almost daily. New techniques are being developed for classroom instruction and advances in technology are simplifying many aspects of the educational environment. Only time will tell how successful all these changes will be in the development of a twentyfirst century society. After teaching for twenty five years, I have some concerns as I witness...

The Changing Face of Education

Let me tell you a saga of instructional change
Which of late tends to keep one amazed...
At the high-tech vocabulary used by those 'pros'
Who have never for TEACHING been praised.

Every year some new 'expert' designs something vague
Which on paper resembles success,
But, when used for instruction in the daily routine,
Ends up looking like something much less.
For the expert's been absent from class now for years
And just thinks that he knows what is best...
While the teacher who integrates these changes each year
Knows such changes will not pass the test-
Of ensuring improvement in student success,
The result of some new point of view,
But only result in frustration severe
In attempting to learn false from true...
For the present-day student still must comprehend
How to USE all the facts that he's learned-
An objective which now he might never attain,
Since the basics need not be discerned.
With the help of computers, his mind need not cope
With the processes which lead to what's best:
He only need memorize the computer vocab-
The machine will then do all the rest!

And so, as he ages, the teacher soon learns
That the road to an "A" has new signs
Which he, as the guide, must begrudgingly use,
Teaching sadly until he resigns.

How sad that many teachers lose their "spark", their "drive" and their desire to "participate". Their plight reminds me of that great song of the 1960's, PUFF, THE MAGIC DRAGON, performed so beautifully by Peter, Paul and Mary.

As a lover of music I have, during the past twenty-five years, composed new lyrics for several songs, most of them in Spanish, to be used for motivation in the classroom. Recently, however, I composed the following lyrics in which I envision MY future through the 'eyes' of PUFF. Are you brave enough to try to sing the following verses? (I know that you know the melody!) And, if you are a teacher, you may even wish to replace my name and my subject area with your own...

Craig, the Spanish Teacher

Craig, the Spanish teacher
Lived near a school
In which he taught for many years,
On days both warm and cool.
And each and ev'ry student
Who came into his class
Enjoyed the human give and take
As he tried his best to pass.

(repeat)

For more than thirty happy years
Craig always did his best,
Encouraging his students-
Motivation did the rest-
And helped each generation
Of kids from 'round the world
To cope with its society
As each young life unfurled.

Craig, the Spanish teacher (etc.)

(repeat)

And when those eager students
Would come into Craig's room,
They'd speak in Spanish ev'ry day,
September until June.
Then one year it happened,
The classroom disappeared...
With TV and computer screens
Replacing, as was feared,
The few remaining teachers
Who loved to be in school.
So Craig no longer came to class,
A fate still viewed as cruel...
For though the children learned a lot
As at the screens they stared,
There was no inspiration from
A source who truly cared.

Craig, the Spanish teacher,
Lived near a school
In which he taught for many years,
On days both warm and cool.

(repeat)

Craig, the Spanish teacher,
LIVES near a school
And he still continues teaching,
On days both warm and cool.

(repeat)

I didn't hear too many of you singing! And singing is a way to help you relax and unwind. These lyrics show that I do have an interest in music. I have been active in singing groups since I was in 7th grade and I continue to enjoy 'musical therapy' today, both at home and in my car.

I also integrate singing into my classroom instruction. On the first day of classes, I ask my students to provide the titles of some of their favorite songs. Then, when time permits (on days when there are shortened classes due to delayed openings, State testing, special assemblies, fire drills, etc.) I encourage the classes to sing. Quite often, I translate the lyrics of popular songs into Spanish so that one outcome of the singing sessions is that of pronunciation reinforcement and practice.

Of all of the songs I have used in class, the most successful has been a Spanish version of THE BANANA BOAT SONG. While the melody line is the same, the lyrics were written to review food vocabulary. They tell of a sailor who comes ashore and goes into a restaurant for breakfast. After writing the new lyrics, I sent to Washington, D.C. and obtained a copyright for them. Then, in 1990, several students who were enrolled in Spanish classes at Cherry Hill EAST AND were also members of several musical groups, volunteered to make a recording of the tune. I made arrangements for a session at a local recording studio and the 'Day-O-Night Singers' produced a tape that is now used by all of the Spanish teachers for a 'fun review' of breakfast vocabulary. Because EGGS are an essential part of any breakfast menu, I titled the song...

Huevos

Hue-vos, Hue -e -e -vos
Huevos revueltos con tocino hoy, (ho-oy)
Hue-, es un hue-, es un hue-, es un hue-,
               es un hue-, es un hue-, -e -e -vo,
Huevos revueltos con tocino hoy.

Ve lo que yo he puesto, gerente,
Huevos revueltos con tocino hoy, (ho-oy)
Un desayuno pa' toda la gente,
Huevos revueltos con tocino hoy.

Ven acá, capitán, mira estos huevos,
Huevos revueltos con tocino ho-oy,
Ven acá, capitán, mira estos huevos,
Huevos revueltos con tocino hoy.

Ve lo que pongo al lado de toda,
Huevos revueltos con tocino ho-oy,
Un vaso grande de jugo de piña,
Huevos revueltos con tocino hoy.

Hue-, es un hue- -vo,
Huevos revueltos con tocino ho-oy,
Hue-, es un hue-, es un hue-, es un hue-, es un hue...
        Huevos revueltos con tocino hoy.

Ve cómo llegan, con té y pan tostado,
Huevos revueltos con tocino ho-oy;
Tú debes gozar de cada alimento,
Huevos revueltos con tocino hoy.

Ve lo que cuesta esta gran comida,
Huevos revueltos con tocino hoy, (ho-oy)
Sólo veinte pesos, con tres de propina,
Huevos revueltos con tocino hoy.

Hue-, es un hue- -vo,
Huevos revueltos con tocino ho-oy,
Hue-, es un hue-, es un -hue-, es un hue-, es un hue- ...
        Huevos revueltos con tocino hoy.

Ven acá, capitán, pide estos huevos,
Huevos revueltos con tocino ho-oy,
Ven acá, capitán, pide estos huevos,
Huevos revueltos con tocino hoy.

Hue-vos , hue- -e -e -vos,
Huevos revueltos con tocino ho-oy,
Hue-, es un hue-, es un hue-, es un hue-,
        es un hue-, es un hue- -e -e -vo,
Huevos revueltos con tocino HOY.

What a great change of pace for the students in class! And what a fantastic experience for those students who had the opportunity to 'perform' in a real recording studio.

There are many extra-curricular activities in any high school that require supervision. The role of faculty adviser is an important one, but is also one that can be very rewarding. Since my first year of teaching at Cherry Hill EAST, in 1968, I have served as adviser to a variety of student groups: a Science-Fiction Club, an Asian Cultural Society, a Foreign Language Literary Society, an Adopt-A-Grandparent program (a community-service program set up with a local Nursing Home) and, of course, the EAST Spanish Club. One ongoing part of my work as adviser has been that of encouraging...

Participation

What can you do
When class is through?
Well don't be blue!
Here's what to do:
PARTICIPATE!

Now, please don't laugh.
For I'm not daft!
Doesn't every craft
Need to be staffed?
PARTICIPATE!

Come onl Let's go!
Let's have a show!
Please don't say "NO",
Join those in the know:
PARTICIPATE!

Can you not see
The fun and glee
For you and me
In activity?
PARTICIPATE!

Have I, in truth, erred?
Are my lines absurd?
Or has someone been spurred
By this one little word...
PARTICIPATE!

I wrote this poem in 1966 to accompany an article for the RUTGERS College Newspaper. In 1991, I put it in the first issue of the EAST Home and School Newsletter for the 1991-1992 school year. As you can probably tell, I will go to great lengths to help motivate students. Fortunately, the students have responded well and have planned many interesting and exciting activities. One such activity was sponsored by the SPANISH CLUB and involved...

Adopting a Child by Mail

The SPANISH CLUB at High School EAST
Adopted a 10-year old
Whose name is Maria Concepcion,
And here her story's told.

The members picked out PARAGUAY
In October, `83,
And completed application forms
(Sent to an agency
That arranges all adoptions
Throughout the Spanish world
For groups and individuals
Who eagerly have hurled
Themselves, and an adoption fee-
In great anticipation
Of years and years of glee-
Into the vast adoption world
Shared by so many now)...
And waited very patiently,
As all of us know how,
To get the address of the child
To whom they soon would write.
(And practiced writing messages,
Morning, noon and night!)

In early 1984
The membership received
A letter from the agency:
Its goal had been achieved!
They wrote a letter to the girl,
Enclosing photographs-
Of EAST and of the membership
At which the Club still laughs.
The child is named MARIA,
Her home, Asuncion,
Her birthday's in October,
Her parents are unknown.

They didn't hear a word from her
Within the next six weeks
So they wrote another letter
(As one who return mail seeks).
They wrote in March and April,
But by the month of June
They still had not received a note...
And school was ending soon.

A call was made to Richmond:
"How come we haven't heard
From our adopted youngster?
We haven't heard a word!"

The group was told that some delays
Will frequently result
When dealing with some countries
(Whether child or young adult)
Because of language problems
Or military rule...
Thus maybe nothing would be heard
Before the end of school.

The Club received a letter
In the middle of July.
And as to such a long delay,
The members found out why:

MARIA's mother had been found
And MARIA moved away...
To live outside Asuncion,
With her mother now to stay.
She still will pay a visit
To the NATIONAL CHILDREN'S HOME
Whenever she can 'get a ride'
From her distant family home.
In Coronel Oviedo
She's now attending class
And, as a third grade student,
NEW friends she will amass.
She hopes to hear a lot from EAST
Within the coming years,
And in her note, she thanked the Club
For sending her some 'cheers'.

The future of the protect
For the membership at EAST
Should prove to be exciting
And that's to say the least!!
The group will keep on writing
To its friend in PARAGUAY
Thus learning of its culture
As all the years go by.

Another exciting activity for the students at EAST has been the yearly publication of a Foreign Language Literary Magazine titled PASSPORT. This publication began in 1989 and was designed to help increase student awareness of the many cultures and languages that are a part of the school community. Let me give you some idea of the work that the students do after classes in order to put together...

Passport: A Celebration of Languages and Cultures

What a great way to showcase world cultures
And the languages spoken in each:
A magazine published by students
Who are proud to be able to teach
About customs and lasting traditions,
From countries all over our world,
In short essays and wonderful poems
Which in PASSPORT are proudly unfurled
So that students may gain an awareness
Of ideas (and images, too)
That prove to be quite universal
When presented for readers to view.

Each student who writes for EAST's PASSPORT
Writes at first in his own native tongue,
Then translates his work into English...
With assistance from friends, old and young.
Each selection is enhanced with great artwork
Done by talented classmates at EAST
And is proofread and carefully typeset,
Then in text form quite carefully pieced.

What a tribute to talented students
Whose achievements are proudly displayed
In an artistic and literary format
To which compliments have recently been paid:
It was honored by the New Jersey Assembly
For honors achieved for its work-
Two National Scholastic citations
And praise for community work!!

But the enjoyment I get as adviser
To these students who are still in their teens
Is watching the work of these 'experts'-
So creative in established routines-
As they seek to enhance understanding
Of the world that we live in today:
I am proud to be part of that process,
So successful in every way!

I have also served as the faculty adviser to a group of students who participate in a very rewarding community service program with residents at a local Nursing Home. The students visit the MERIDIAN Healthcare Center in Voorhees, New Jersey, two afternoons each week for an hour and a half. While members are sharing their experiences with the residents, they discover that they are also learning a great deal about daily life in earlier decades of the 20th century. The student group was the focus of a feature story in the <u>Courier-Post</u> newspaper in August, 1993 and I was honored as 1993 Volunteer of the Year by the New Jersey Association of Healthcare Facilities in October, 1993 for my work with the group. Participation in this program has increased from 20 to more than 100 in the past four years and is an activity that lives up to its name...

Adopt - A - Grandparent
A Community Service Program

An ADOPT - A - GRANDPARENT program
Can be very rewarding indeed:
Students willing to share
And showing they care
About Nursing Home residents in need ...
Of someone to talk with on topics
Of int'rest to them and to teens;
Or to do arts and crafts,
Or tell jokes filled with laughs ...
As they relive some memorable scenes
Or a childhood in days very diff'rent
From the ones being faced by our youth,
And in words often wise
(Which at times hypnotize)
Take us back to the days of THEIR youth!

For the students, the visits are helpful
As they learn how their world came to be...
And the time that they share
With the residents there
Bring rewards they could never foresee!!

Although all of these extra-curricular duties require a lot of time, the satisfaction that comes from watching the students grow and mature makes that extra time well worthwhile. My experiences with the residents at the Nursing Home have given me a greater appreciation of the time and effort given by so many dedicated volunteers at area hospitals and nursing facilities. We all should set aside some time for this type of community service. We all should take a minute from our busy schedules to give...

Thanks to the Volunteers

There are many auxiliary groups in our land
That dedicate hours of time
To that marvelous goal
Of cheering some soul
Who from serious illness must climb.
It's a difficult mountain, holding dangers unknown,
With which every patient must cope.
But the volunteer force-
Always smiling, of course-
Helps support every 'climber' with hope.
For it's these willing workers who give
Or their time
Without thought of how much it is worth.
Their reward every day
Comes from deeds WITHOUT pay
Which result in some patient's rebirth.
They work very proudly for the good of all those
Who need many things to keep "livin'."
And though they are few,
They do what they do
In thanks for what they have been given.

Let's all tip our hats to these volunteers
Who give of their time without fees.
What they do as a group
Has helped many recoup...
Of them all we're as proud as can be!!!

So ends part two of my journey. The information presented reflects a lot of hard work, but also describes the joy that comes from working with and for the youth of our generation. And when I am the recipient of a letter from a former student who has taken the time to inform me of his or her success after graduation, it gives me the feeling that I made the correct choice for a career.

Part Three

**People, Places and Things
The Preservation of Memories**

<u>**The Past**</u>

In this section of my journey I shall provide you, the reader, with some tips on how to keep the present alive long after it has become the past. To begin, emphasis will be placed on some of the changes I have seen taking place over the past three decades. I shall also speculate a little on what happens to all of those great ideas that are perceived by our senses and that enter into our "memory".

Sit back and relax (if you can) and follow me as I investigate some of the incredible changes that have occurred in our society: changes that are often taken for granted. I shall begin with a description of the changes that have taken place on the faces of our clocks and watches. Of course, I am referring to ...

Hands of Time

I looked upon my kitchen wall
To see if I'd perchance recall
The visual show, in silent mime,
Of those two gleaming hands of Time
Which travel through each day and night,
Affording me some great delight
As, roaming through the clock's bright face,
They run Time's never-ending race.

But Man has loosed those hands of Time,
Replacing them - Oh, what a crime!-
With numbers, blinking off and on,
To calculate how Time has gone.
The beauty of the face of Time,
Together with each hour's chime,
Is now devoid of charming sights:
There's only clicking, both days and nights.

Yes! Computerized precision strikes again! And the watches on our wrists even beep to ensure that accuracy is being maintained... at all times! And with the changes in timekeeping methods comes the elimination of individuality, for all timepieces are beginning to look alike.

Of course, the same sequence of events seems to be taking place on the fashion scene. At times, it is difficult to know whether the person whom you are watching is male or female, the result of some recent...

Changes

While walking through the Mall today, I saw a funny sight:
A boy had had his ear pierced, for who knows what delight!
And as I looked around the Mall, I could not help but see
That girls were wearing blue jeans where skirts oft' used to be!
As I continued on my way, I passed a beauty shop...
With more young men than ladies getting perms with curls on top!!

These changes seem so strange to me; I must be growing old.
At least I've found the perfect shop where necklaces are sold!

There are, of course, other changes which occur in our lives: changes caused by the aging process, rather than by innovations in our society. One of these changes may cause us to frown more than smile. I am referring to those incredible...

Dental Changes

I could hardly believe it.
It couldn't be true!
How could I have cavities
In three sets of two?
The last time they checked them,
Not one could be found.
And now -- three years later --
They appear to abound.
There are four on the top set
And two more below,
And a crack in a filling
That to me gives great woe.
I feel like a youngster
Who's just heard the news:
"Three more visits for fillings.
Now don't sing the blues."

I guess I'm just aging
And falling apart,
Though my fam'ly physician
Says I have a strong heart.
My blood pressure's normal
And I'm not overweight;
My legs are not swollen...
And my hearing is great!
Of course, I need glasses
To help me to see,
But today that seems normal:
There are millions like me.

So what's gonna happen
In the years yet to come?
Will I need to wear dentures,
Or my food have to gum??
Who knows what may happen,
But of one thing I'm sure:
If my smile becomes ugly,
It's because of the cure!!

You noticed that I mentioned that I wear glasses. I am grateful for this 'invention', since it permits me to observe and enjoy the world around me. But, as I age, I often wonder what will happen to all of those sharp images (such as those that appear during a beautiful sunset). It is quite possible that, some day, those brilliant images may turn to...

Embers of a Dying Flame

When the stars begin to twinkle
In the brilliant skies above,
And Moon beams hypnotize us all,
Our thoughts soon turn to love.
Our dreams convey us into worlds
Where true beauty we can see;
Where sight transforms our senses
Into happiness and glee.

But what occurs on cloudy nights
When those stars we can not see?
When moonlight can not penetrate
The clouds and bring us glee?
We sit in darkness, all alone,
And remember starlit skies:
Our mem'ry helps us to recall
Those fantastic nights gone by.
Thus sight provides us chances
To explore 'The Great Beyond',
And travel to some great new worlds
Of which we're all so fond.

Don't take your sight for granted!
Enjoy those moonlit skies!
For cataracts and loss of sight
Are like a cloud disguise
Which takes away the Present,
With its never-ending change,
And forces on its victims
The need to re-arrange
All those precious moonlight ventures
To worlds of ecstasy-
With constant repetition
Of historic fantasy.

And if, as vision disappears,
Our memory starts to fade,
Life changes to Existence
In a world of constant shade.
Thus we are left with remnants
Of the real-world tapestry,
Sewn together with mere shadows
From our lost reality.

Have you noticed what a fascinating trait the MEMORY is? It helps to tie the Past to the Present. It also forms part of our individual personalities, since each person may recall a particular event from a different perspective. But what happens to all of those facts and figures and images that enter into our 'memory'? Why is it that some people remember certain facts and can recall certain images, while others who have experienced the same situation can NOT? If only someone could do a study on...

The Fate of 'Lost' Ideas

As all of us develop, day by day,
Throughout our lengthy lives,
We collect a treasure of fine ideas
On which our mem'ry thrives;
For everything we see and do
(In work, as well as play)
Results in new experiences,
With thoughts in fine array.

But what becomes of most of these
As through the brain they pass?
(For often we can not recall
Some date, or site, or lass!)
Do they remain quite hidden
In the caverns of the mind...
Just waiting for the mem'ry bank
Their proper niche to find?
Or do they simply penetrate
Without attempts to stay,
And exit through some secret door
To quickly sneak away??

> I often try to bring to mind
> Some mem'ry from my past,
> And find that much is missing
> To make the mem'ry last.
> Perhaps some day I'll find the 'key'
> Which opens wide my mind:
> That treasure chest of fine ideas
> Of days long left behind.
> But if, by chance, there's nothing there...
> Except some empty space...
> I'll realize that thoughts escape
> And into TIME do race!

How can a person keep important information from "escaping"? I have implemented a variety of techniques in order to prevent such data from disappearing into the mists of the past. I purchase a diary every year and keep a record of all of my daily activities in Spanish. Each day's summary includes what I consider to be important developments in the community, the country and the world. I also list the names of those famous individuals who have passed away and of those who have been honored for special achievements. In the decade of the 1970's, I began composing a poetic "calendar summary" for each year, thinking that such a project would help events of the past 'stay alive'. I thought you might enjoy looking back with me at several verses taken from these poetic memoirs. How many of these names do you remember from that...

Double Digit Year of 1977

Many famous persons,
From many walks of life,
Began their homeward journey
After years of fruitful 'strife'.
Their names will live forever
In the hearts of those who cared,
For these were gifted talents
Who to entertain us dared.

They included CHARLIE CHAPLIN,
A comic world-renowned,
As well as GUY LOMBARDO
With his New Year's Ev'ning sound.
The crooner named BING CROSBY,
Who made "White Christmas" live,
And the legend ELVIS PRESLEY,
Who had so much to give
To the world of 'Rock 'n Rollin'"...
In the famous 'Hound Dog' style...
And whose lyrics and gyrations
Entertained us with a smile.

The actress named JOAN CRAWFORD,
Who lived each part she played
In movies for five decades
That for her fans were made.
And who could forget dear GROUCHO
With cigar and famous brows,
Who entertained for decades
And often took no bows.
Our famous servants BUELAH
And Jack Benny's ROCHESTER,
Who gave folks fun-filled moments
From Nome to Chichester.

It's these great entertainers,
Who gave us times of cheer,
Whom we will long remember
Through each succeeding year.

What an amazing list of members from the "Who's Who of Entertainment".

On a personal note, that year of 1977 will always be remembered because it marked the beginning of my 'romance' with "IVY." I still shutter when I read these lines, written on December 28, 1977...

>A poison ivy syndrome-
>From which my right arm swelled,
>And which spread throughout my body
>Before it could be quelled-
>Attacked me this October
>After I had touched this weed
>While cutting back some hedges,
>Which of trimming were in need.
>For SIX LONG WEEKS I suffered
>From a tendency to scratch;
>I had to take much medicine
>And my arm each night to patch!

So now you know WHY I decided to call that enchanting poem about my romance: AN IRRITATING LOVE STORY!!!

Do you remember that these were some of the headlines for the...

1978 Calendar Year

>Around the world, the scene was bleak,
>With riots building every week.
>Iran and Italy led the list,
>With Israel and Egypt not to be missed...
>For the latter nations promised peace,
>But border struggles would not cease.
>And at year's end, with GOLDA dead,
>SADAT and BEGIN would not be led
>To sign a pact to end the strife.
>But that's a symbol of our life...
>For murder, rape and death abound
>Each time we stop and look around.

In local news, OTTO KRUPP made news for EAST
By stabbing MUIR just like a beast
And then, when he was granted bail,
Took his boat and away did sail.

But in GUYANA seven hundred died
By committing 'Kool-Aid' suicide.
And near Chicago, thirty boys were found,
Raped and buried all around -
In crawl space and in nearby stream-
By a maniac who had a scheme:
To hire teens for sexual glee,
Then kill them quietly so none would see.

If we take a look at the headlines in 1993, it would appear that, indeed, some things NEVER change. In that same year, 1978, I traveled to Cancun, Mexico, where I spent a week of my summer vacation. It was there that I first heard about Timesharing. In November, I received an invitation to attend a Timesharing presentation in Atlantic City (I was at a local bowling alley for my weekly arm-strengthening exercises!). That invitation proved to be the beginning of a fabulous 'relationship' (that will be described in more detail in Part Four of my journey). My calendar poem for 1978 included the following references to this new and exciting 'adventure'...

This summer brought a lively tune
Played by a band in new CANCUN.
I spent eight days in Yucatan
And saw remains of early Man.
I spent much time on beaches white
And spoke in Spanish, day and night.
And when, at last, I did depart,
CANCUN was buried in my heart.
For rest and beauty can be seen
Along its beaches, white and clean...
A place where life appears to be
A Paradise for men like me.

One place I saw while I was there
Announced a plan which seemed quite fair:
You buy a suite or villa grand
For several weeks (for vacations planned),
Then, if you'd like to switch your time
And spend it in another clime,
You travel to each place you like,
But hotel rates they cannot hike.
So, in December, I became
A member of a hotel chain
By joining with the RCI,
As I a suite of rooms did buy.
The place I bought for just eight grand
Was at the shore, quite near the sand.
Atlantic City was the spot:
PARK LANE SUITE was what I bought.

So at year's end I wrote away
To learn of sites where I might stay
Next summer when I'm free to roam-
Perhaps to places far from home.

What a great investment! There were NO casino-hotels in Atlantic City when I purchased two weeks of Timesharing on Illinois Avenue. My investment more than doubled within four years after my purchase!!

In 1980, all of the information included in the summary dealt with summer activities and headlines. This was what was happening during...

The Summer of 1980

As my summer quickly ended
With more heat and hazy air,
I went to see a movie
Which could clearly make you stare:
The second part of STAR WARS,
With Darth Vader and his 'friends'
Attacking Luke Skywalker
Before the movie ends.

In the real world IRAN is still holding
Fifty hostages in tow,
And Presidential candidates
Are now all on the go.
The SHAH OF IRAN died slowly
As the summer slipped away,
And humorist SAMUEL LEVINSON
Had had his final say.

My personal adventures during that summer introduced me to life in a real 'Paradise': MAUI, HAWAII. And though I had left my heart in Cancun, Mexico two years earlier, I would leave my soul forever blowing in the tradewinds after my Timeshare Exchange to the MAUI SUNSET Resort on the Kihei coast of Maui...

It all began quite quickly
On the 24th of June
When I took off for Hawaii -
Twas the week of the full moon.
I stayed at the MAUI SUNSET
In Suite B 515
And Mom and I just rested
While enjoying the MAUI scene.
We visited Lahaina,
With its ancient Banyon Tree,
And had a buffet 'bruncheon'
Eating five desserts with glee.
We dined at the HYATT MAUI
By a pool and waterfall.
We watched both swans
And penguins
And strolled through its shopping mall.

We shopped in Wailea,
As well as in Kihei,
And bought some "Blue Hawaii",
But not a single lei.

The weather was just perfect,
With a lovely windward breeze.
Twas a climate quite delightful
Which one not often sees.
But Paradise is special
And Time just flies away,
Thus bringing back reality
After one week and a day.

From that summer on, my favorite expression has been: HERE TODAY, GONE TO MAUI. Three weeks after returning from Maui, I took off on another Timeshare Exchange to the quaint Mexican town of San Miguel Allende, located some 200 miles north of Mexico City. What a trip filled with surprises! Not only did I 'bump into' the grandmother of one of my students while walking through the outdoor market, but I experienced the real 'adventure' of traveling by rail in Mexico. I left my room at 10:30 am to get to the train station 'on time' (by noon, the time indicated on the schedule as the arrival hour for the train coming from northern Mexico and headed for Mexico City). The rest, as they say, is history...

My train ride back to Mexico
Was almost an ordeal,
For it lasted THIRTEEN hours...
And I didn't have a meal!
I waited for five hours
Before the train arrived,
And learned, just after boarding,
That no food nor drink survived
The delays the train had witnessed
On its trip to SAN MIGUEL...
So I ate just five lifesavers
Till I got to my hotel.
BUT... food could not be purchased
In the hotel dining room
At 1:30 in the morning!!! ...
So I went straight to my room.

What a summer! Then, on December 31st, I wrote several additional verses that dealt with world events AND local sports excitement...

Mount St. Helen's covered us all with ash,
While Italian earthquakes many lives did smash.
The Russians invaded Afghanistan,
While the Mideast Peace talks were nearly banned.

In the sports world the PHILLIES fin'ly won the big game,
And are now the heroes of World Series fame!
The Winter Olympics were held in New York,
With Lake Placid medals rewards for good work....
BUT the Summer Olympics were not quite as great,
Since America's athletes did NOT participate.

The EAGLES in football are now 12 and 4
And head coach Vermeil is hoping for more
As he enters the Playoffs with his talented team...
In hopes of attaining that SUPER BOWL 'Gleam'!

As you see, I found this project of writing a 'calendar poem' for each year very entertaining AND informative. And such a written record does help 'jog' the memory. Unfortunately, during the 1980's I failed to continue maintaining notes on important events and, as a result, no poetic summaries were written. My excuse has been that "TIME" did not allow me to 'reread' all of my daily diary entries at the end of the year, due to other responsibilities an instructor and adviser. Some excuse! It sounds like those incredible lyrics in the song CATS IN THE CRADLE, made so famous by the late Harry Chapin.

Without an organized record of our 'great moments' in life, TIME tends to erode the sharpness of the images. In the summer of 1993, while attending a fabulous Hawaiian show in Maui (where the stars can be shining brightly while 'pineapple rain' is falling closeby), I wrote this somewhat sad commentary on those...

Magical Moments in Time

I shall never forget that evening!
There are so many reasons why:
There were dancers who swayed,
While a band deftly played,
As a singer sang a soft lullaby.

As I sat at a table beside her,
The stars watched us both from on high
And reflected their light
In her eyes, blue and bright,
Like soft rain on the cars going by.

Was it she that I'll always remember,
Who had so many stories to tell?
Or was it the light
On the stage, shining bright,
That performed with the dancers so well??

A moment in Time is so precious
That its memory will last through the years.
But what makes it endure
Is that certain 'allure'...
That with Time only brings on the tears.
For the details drift off into cobwebs
That prevent us from making it last.
What that moment had meant,
And the meaning it sent,
Are just shadows now lost in the past!

Another technique used by most of us to relive precious moments in our lives is that of photography. Photographs, slides and videos enable us to recall many enjoyable experiences from our youth. Unfortunately, many of us take pictures of events and people and places WITHOUT identifying them once they have been developed. After 15 or 20 years, these visual images become only shadows of reality, because we forget where they were taken, when they were taken and, in some situations, why they were taken. We often ask ourselves why our relatives didn't label family photos... and then don't label our own!

I find that labeling photos with a poetic summary helps identify the situations AND provides some 'emotional contact' with the person, place or thing. Let me take you on a short trip down MY memory lane and introduce you to some events that resulted in poetic description.

As anyone who works in a school or large office building knows, the hub of communications is centered at the desk or office of the receptionist. Often taken for granted, he or she is the person responsible for taking messages, forwarding calls, answering incredible questions, giving directions AND trying to survive at the same time. It takes a special person to serve as a receptionist and in many cases, the value of that individual is not recognized until AFTER he or she retires or moves away. Cherry Hill EAST had such a charismatic personality. When she retired after more than 20 years of service, I put together a 'little' 67-page tribute entitled: FRANKIE LOWER: THIS IS YOUR LIFE. It contained photos taken from Yearbooks during her career at EAST and even a 'quiz': "Guess the Year!" with some incredible Yearbook photos that she had to try to identify... photos of the 'receptionist in action'. Her name was Frances, but everyone knew her as "Frankie". In June, 1991, I presented Frankie with the 'diary' and a selection entitled...

Frankie

There's a place that I know in a high school
In a township that is named Cherry Hill...
It's the HEART of a great institution
In which learning has become a great thrill.
And the person who keeps that HEART beating
Very often at times of great strain
Is receptionist queen FRANKIE LOWER,
Whose talents help the staff to stay sane.
She dedicates each working hour
To the job that she truly enjoys...
With the help of a Muppet named 'Kermit',
Many 'turkeys' and, of course, girls and boys.
Always smiling in spite of the problems
That pop up without warning each day
(Parents' questions on changes in schedules,
Teachers' memos, election displays),
Frankie's always a model of greatness
As she works at EAST's 'central control',
Working wonders with the 'fabulous' switchboard:
Very few would enjoy Frankie's role!!

FRANKIE LOWER retires this summer,
Though her presence will ALWAYS be there:
Thanks so much for your skill AND your patience-
May your horizons forever be fair!!!

Every time I read those lines, some exciting situations from the past come clearly into view... all of the extension cords sticking through the Communications Office window on Election Day; the adorable little 'gifts' that were given to Frankie by staff and students over the years; the lunch bags and pairs of glasses lining the counter in front of the switchboard.

Another 'farewell composition' was written in June of 1992, when one of the employees of the MERIDIAN Healthcare Center left her position in order to return to school full time and complete her studies. She worked as one of the activities coordinators at the nursing home and was always willing to take time to help out the members of the EAST Adopt-A-Grandparent group when they had questions, etc. Her departure brought to mind the image of a butterfly, flying off to another flower-filled site. Therefore, I presented her with a set of ceramic butterflies and a poem entitled....

An AAG Farewell Message to Jean

Oh JEAN, you'll soon be taking flight
And going back to school.
We know you'll be a great success,
You've got the perfect tool:
A great approach to daily chores
That helps to overcome
Those moments of uncertainty
Which make some people glum.

We'll miss your smile and friendly words
Which made our weekly trips
A meaningful experience...
Thanks for those <u>timely</u> tips!!

We're sending you these butterflies
To guide you on your way
To great success and happiness
In all you do each day.
For just as they emerged to fly
From caterpillars small,
Dear JEAN, <u>you</u> now will fly away
To heed that distant call
Of challenges and, yes, of dreams,
That guide us on our way
As down the Road of Life we go
Through each and ev'ry day.

This parting gift does symbolize
What we have learned so well:
That transformation oh, so fine
Which starts with "show and tell"
For, as we talked with residents
Each Friday afternoon,
We found ourselves to be transformed;
Released from our 'cocoon'!
And, just as these bright butterflies,
We've taken on new form
That brightens up our daily life
And makes us feel real 'warm'.

There's not much more that we can say,
These lines have said it all.
WE'LL. MISS YOU AT MERIDIAN !!!....
So don't forget to call!
And when you ve reached that next plateau
Oh please, don't hesitate
To send a note to AAG
So we can celebrate
And share with you that great success
That Life will give to you,
As through the years you 'flutter on'
And make those dreams come true!!

    I hope that these lines have communicated some of the 'joy' associated with volunteer work with residents in a Nursing Home. The students in the Adopt-A-Grandparent program have come to realize the many benefits associated with community service and with sharing with others.

    As I have already mentioned, I enjoy singing. I have participated in a variety of musical organizations ever since I was a student at Audubon High School in Audubon, New Jersey. A truly exciting event took place at Audubon High in June, 1993 (30 years after my graduation). A special 'Alumni Concert' was organized to honor Mr. Richard M. Smith, the Music

Director at the school. Mr. Smith spent his entire teaching career at AHS and was planning to retire after 33 years as an educator. During his tenure, the AHS Concert Choir travelled to Europe on four occasions for a musical tour. Mr. Smith also served as Director of the All-State Chorus and was recognized as one of those rare individuals who loved working with the young generation. Evidence of his influence on his students was clearly seen in the response to the invitation to participate in the special concert. More than 200 graduates took part, some coming from as far away as Texas and California for the weekend to thank Mr. Smith for all that he had done for them. A special program was handed out to all in attendance and one page included a poem that I had written for the event...

A Tribute to Mr. Richard M. Smith

What a wonderful musical reunion
Has been planned for you tonight:
You'll enjoy a two-part concert
That will be a sheer delight!
It begins with the regular program
With the students, grades 7-12,
And ends with a trip down memory lane
As into the past we'll delve
For a joyous alumni performance
With a choir some two hundred strong
Dating back to the early sixties...
Richard Smith has been with us that long??!

Yes, indeed! And we're all very happy
To be part of this tribute sincere
To a man who has been so important,
In his long and successful career,
To the Audubon High School tradition
That's reflected in all that he's done.

Richard Smith, here's to YOU, our Director!
In our hearts you're indeed NUMBER ONE !!!

I still live in Audubon... and have lived in the same house my entire life. As a result, I grew up watching all of the Philadelphia sports teams in action. My favorite sport is baseball and I have followed the PHILLIES for nearly half a century. When I was a player in the local Little League, my coach even gave me the nickname SMOKY because my last name was the same as that of SMOKY BURGESS, the catcher for the PHILLIES. Within the last decade, two events occurred involving athletes who had played for the Philadelphia PHILLIES. The first was the retirement of the superstar third baseman of the team, Michael Jack Schmidt. When he retired, I wrote a poem in tribute to his career and sent it to the team announcers, Harry Kalas and Richie Ashburn (in my mind, the best active baseball commentators in the game). The poem was entitled...

Michael Jack Schmidt

Harry Kalas was saddened,
Richie Ashburn was too,
When a great baseball legend
Announced he was through.
Mike Schmidt was in San Diego
On the 29th day in May
When he announced he would retire:
Who could ever forget that day!

Schmidt played for the 'Fightin' Phillies'
For nearly eighteen years
As the renowned gold-glove third basemen
Who stood alone among his peers!
He had always been a PHILLIE
And that had made him proud...
Though once he wore a long black wig
As 'protection' from the crowd.

Mike Schmidt's a true Hall of Famer
And there is one thing for sure:
His famous number 20
In Philadelphia will long endure
As a symbol of 'Schmitty's' greatness
Throughout a fantastic career!!
Let's honor our "Philly legend"
With a wave and with a cheer!!

I shall never forget the Autograph Night held by the wives of the Phillies two years ago when MIKE SCHMIDT personally signed a copy of this tribute. WOW! The poem was written on June 23, 1989.

The second 'headline' involving a member of a PHILLIES team was not a happy one. It dealt with the difficulties being faced by the superstar PETE ROSE, one of the players on the 1980 WORLD SERIES CHAMPIONSHIP TEAM. For some reason, my mind kept thinking about "Roses are red, Violets are blue" as I listened to the many reports about the gambling problems in Mr. Rose's career. The result was this poem, that was also written on June 23, 1989...

The Wilted Rose

The Rose who's a Red
May soon suffer the 'Blues'....
From his betting on baseball
He'll receive his just dues.

For the great fans of baseball
Rose's story is sad:
He's the game's greatest hitter,
But his gambling was bad!

He now manages the Reds team
And has done very well,
Though the courts are now saying
That from Glory he fell
By pursuing his betting
On the game he loves best...
And with bets on his own team,
As well as the rest!

Though Rose was a Red
When the skies were clear Blue,
His future's now cloudy and
His career will be through.
HALL OF FAME recognition
May never come true
For the Rose who's a Red.....
What a sad tale, but true!

What a sad commentary on one of the greatest players to ever play the game! Only the future will tell what the fate of Mr. Rose will be with reference to the Hall of Fame. Most fans will always remember Mr. 'Charlie Hustle' as a player who gave them some lasting memories during a truly remarkable career.

What a fantastic way to bring back some great memories!! But not all memories are happy ones. In my personal life, several situations were filled with anxiety and sadness. These, too, were described in verse because, at least for me, their impact on my daily life was as important as that provided by happier moments.

One of these events occurred in late 1986. One of my aunts, a teacher in the Camden, New Jersey school system for 41 years, had just undergone the traumatic moment in life of moving from her home into a Nursing facility. After only two weeks in the facility, she suffered a stroke that left her 'brain dead'. Nevertheless, she was kept alive, thanks to modern technology, for another six weeks. On Christmas Day, 1986, I described the situation as...

Paradise Postponed

How does one differentiate (at least within his mind)
Between a living body and an angel, oh so kind?
The major change is physical to spiritual in shape
And, yes, there are those lovely wings which offer it escape
From physical imprisonment to soulful ecstasy...
The angel hovers in the mist as lovely form, so free!

My Aunt, whose name is CLARA, has approached this ecstasy,
But modern plastic tubings refuse to set her free.
Her spirit longs to fly on high with newly tested wings,
And yet is still imprisoned by tubes and vials and rings...
Her respiration constant to an artificial beat,
Conveyed throughout her body, from her eyelids to her feet!

The Lord had chosen Paradise at the age of 82,
But Man had chosen LIMBO... for at least a week or two.
Her family asked for Freedom as it uttered this request:
"She surely won't learn how to fly if shackled to this nest,
And all who truly love her believe that she must soar.....
So please remove the shackles and release her Spirit's moor!
Postponing her first day of flight into God's Paradise
Is cruel punishment indeed, with Heaven now in sight".

But as I write this short review of 'Paradise Postponed',
The doctors have not listened, their actions thus condoned.
And what of Dear Aunt CLARA, awaiting her new wings? ...
Perhaps the wait won't be too long, and so to life she clings.

    When Clara retired from teaching in 1963 she was making $7100.00 a year- AFTER 41 YEARS IN EDUCATION!!! I'll never forget the expression on her face when she found out that I was going to make more than $13,000.00 during my first year of teaching at EAST!
    We all have witnessed many mysterious and wonderful events in our lifetime -- events that bring us joy and, quite often, surprise us. If we train ourselves to become better observers of our environment, we will find even more opportunities to "exercise" the senses as well as the body.

Owning a pet can be very rewarding. My favorite pet is a dog and, being a Spanish teacher, I called my 'little' Beagle

Pancho

PANCHO is the dog I own.
He loves to chew a rawhide bone.
But when I leave him all alone,
From sadness he will cry and moan.

He loves to hunt the wily hare,
And at small birds he loves to stare.
And when the apples start to fall,
He treats them like a rubber ball...
By playing with them in his paws,
Then squeezing 'em within his jaws.
And when he wants some food to eat,
He sits up on his sturdy 'seat'
And stately begs, with forepaws crossed,
For any little tidbits tossed.

He likes to soak up lots of sun,
But from a bath he'll always run!
And when it's to the vet he goes...
He shakes, from tail up to his nose!

PANCHO is a Beagle fair
With white and black and tannish hair.
I got him as a tiny pup,
But 'little' PANCHO's now grown up.
His velvet coat is soft and fine:
I sure am glad that PANCHO's mine!!

PANCHO lived for nearly 16 years and I could write an entire book about all of the adventures we shared together. What a great companion!

I mentioned that photography is one way to preserve memories. I thought you might enjoy seeing PANCHO in action. Following the set of photos is a tribute to this unique personality, highlighting the events pictured.

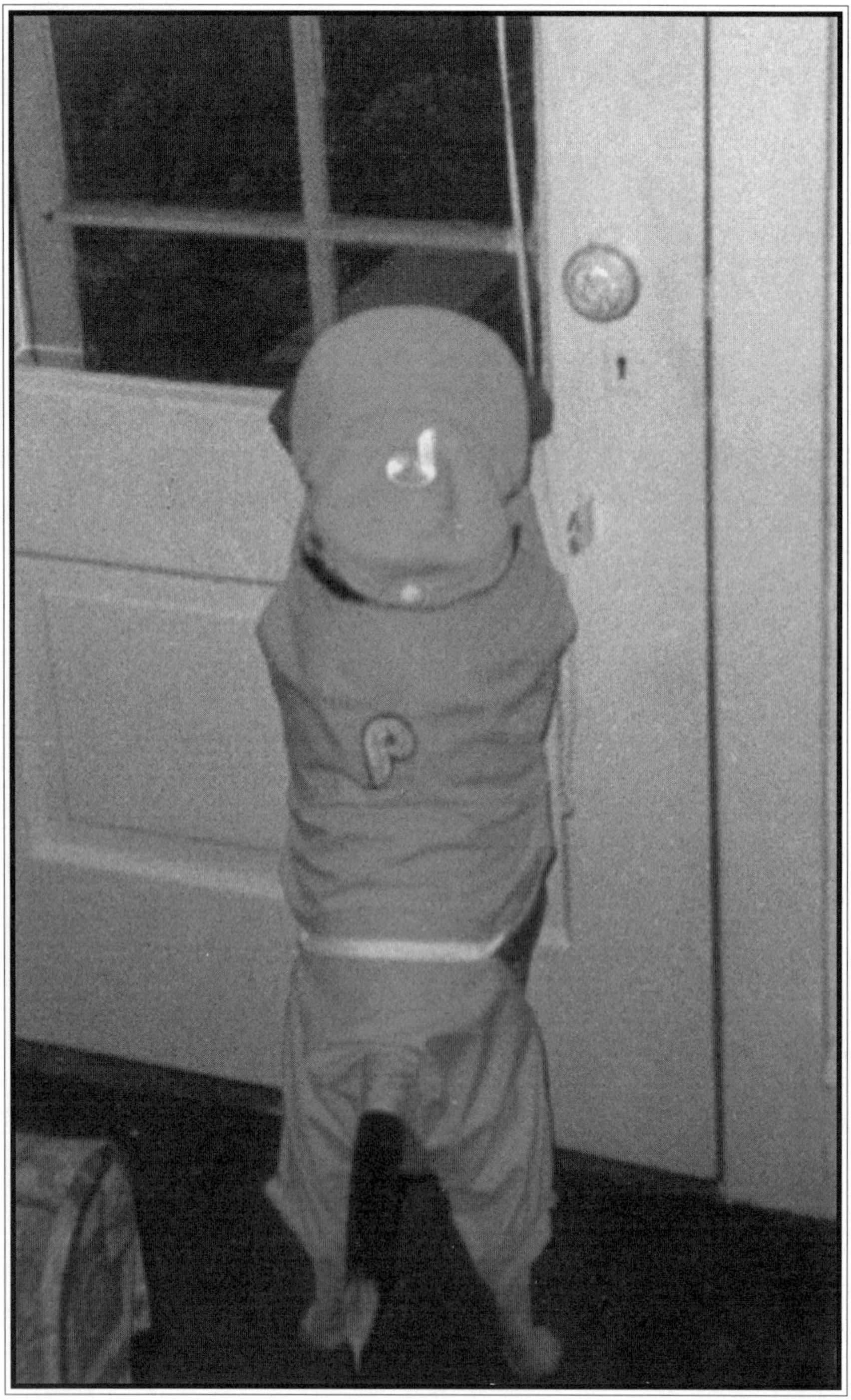

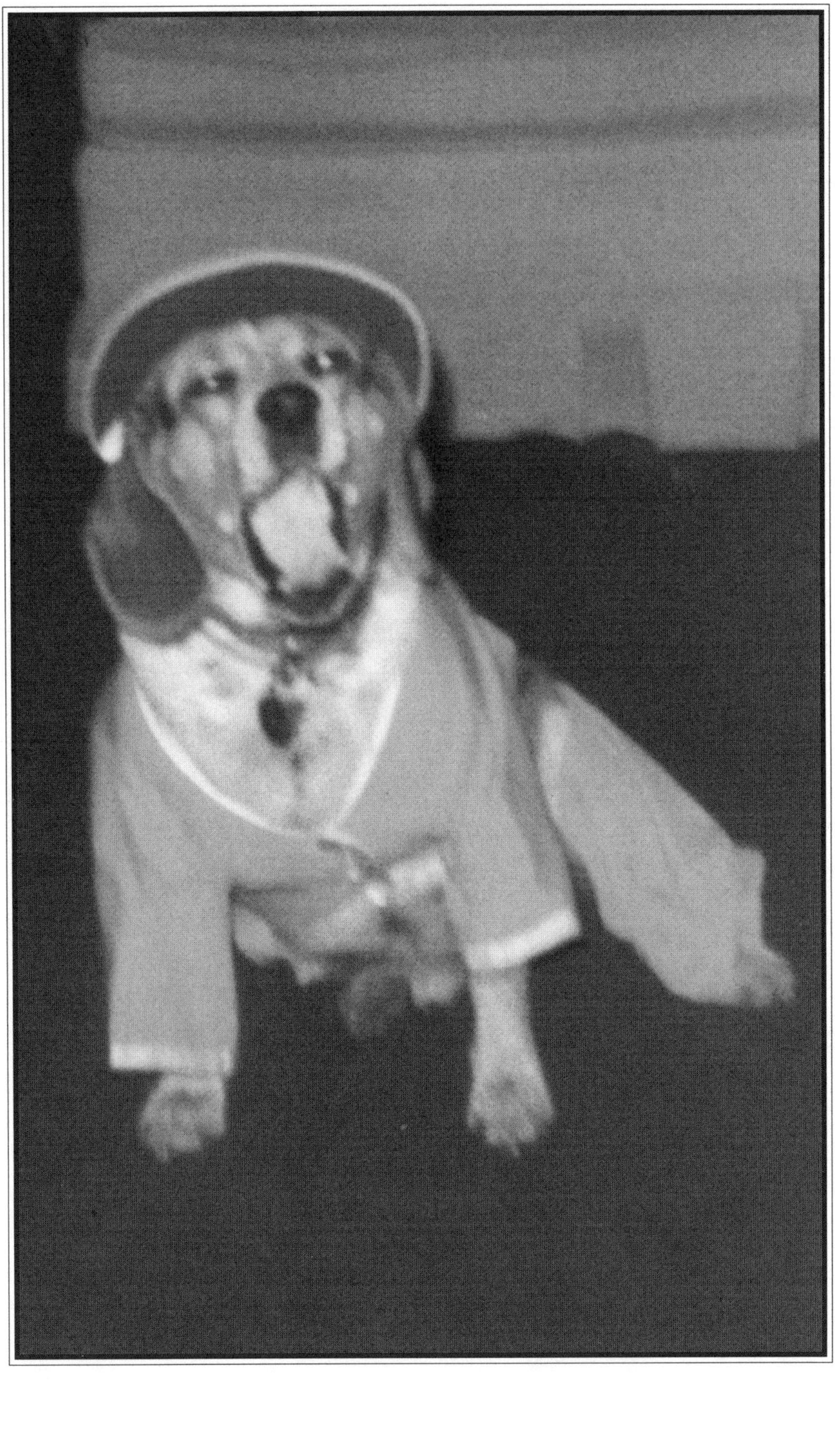

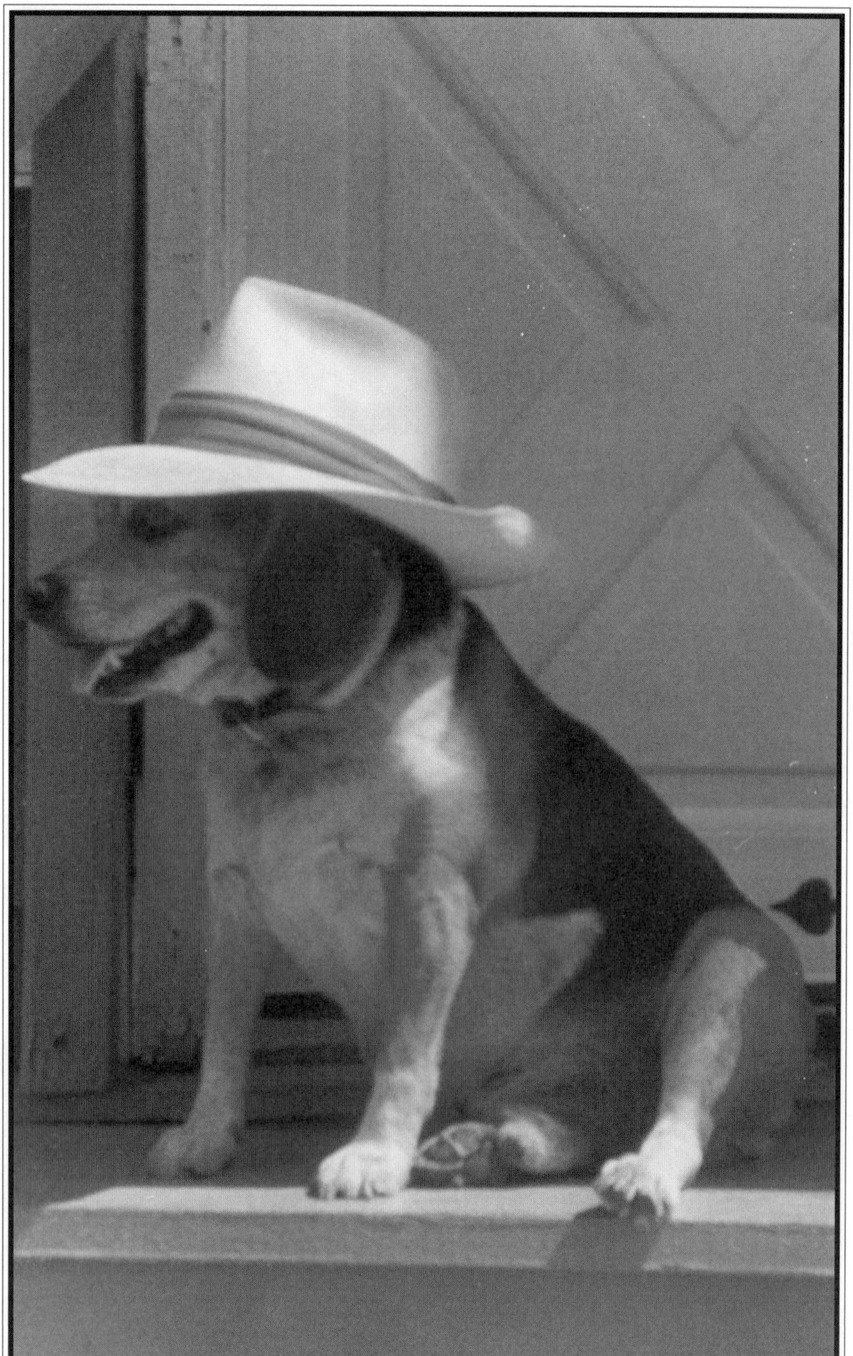

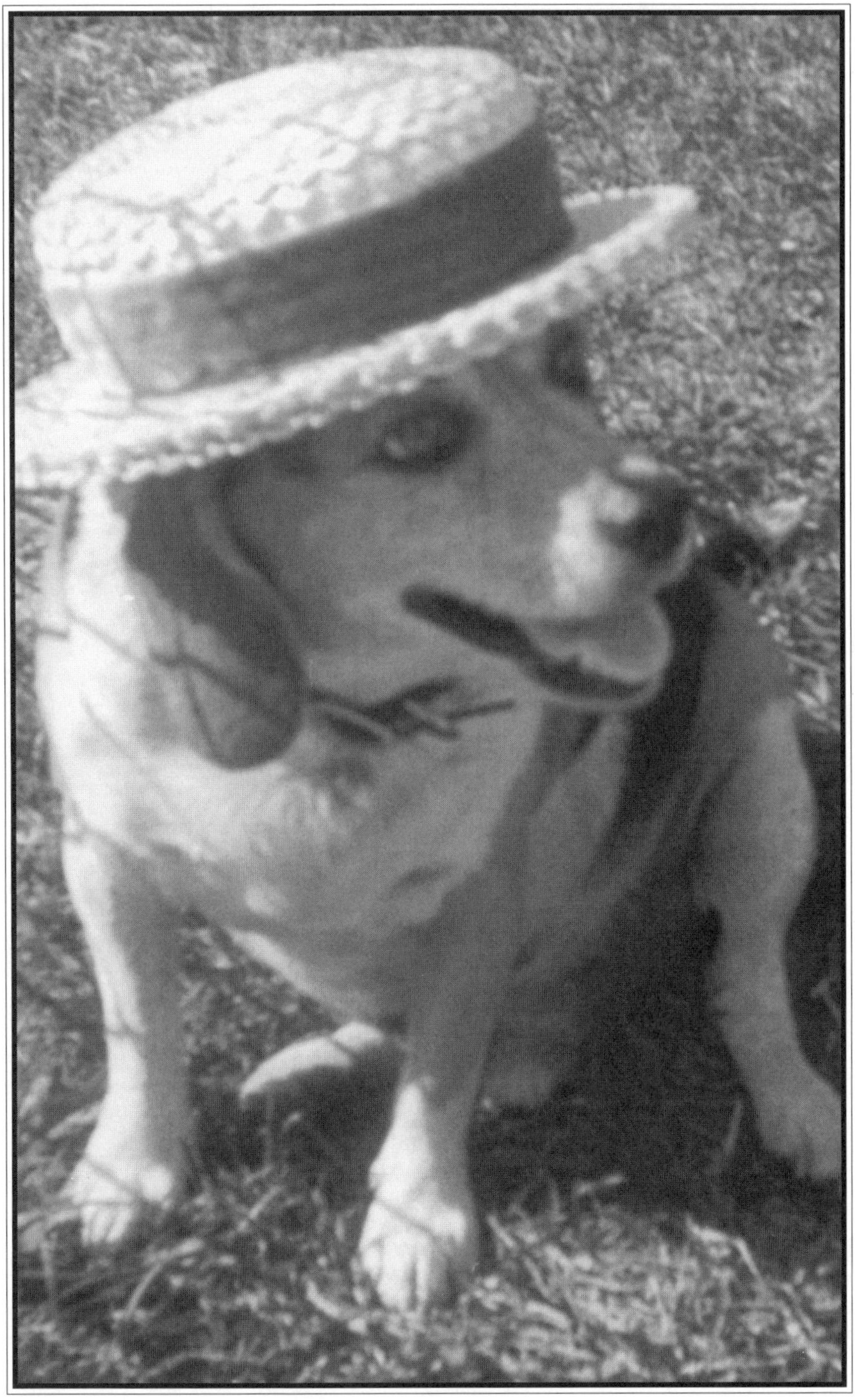

When PANCHO passed away on February 7, 1983, I wrote a poetic summary of his life so that I would always be able to recall some of those 'fun' moments we shared...

Pancho

How to begin a tribute to PANCHO
My adorable little Beagle
Who, after sixteen years in Audubon,
At last became so feeble
That on the 7th day of February,
With a blanket of snow all around,
I took him to the local vet
And to his final resting ground.

We found him in a shelter
When he was only one year old:
An adorable puppy of black white and brown
Who stole our hearts with his nose so cold!

He served as Dad's companion
For nearly two full years
Preferring Dad's lap to his own small bed,
Perhaps because Dad rubbed his ears.
And when Dad died from cancer
On Father's Day in '72,
PANCHO kept looking everywhere-
For at least a month or two-
In efforts to locate his faithful friend
With whom he spent much time,
And appearing to be quite puzzled-
He disappeared without reason or rhyme.

PANCHO suffered from minor epileptic attacks
And from a neck ailment severe.
But, worst of all, was his loss of sight
And his ability to clearly hear.

But his lengthy life with Ruth and Craig
Brought moments of enormous joy...
As he begged with great skill for a 'yummy'
Or rolled over on his cute squeaky toy.

He was very well-known in the neighborhood
And once even appeared in the news
When he wore his famous VOTE COAT
Urging all from the candidates to choose.
He also had his own PHILLIES suit
Which he won from Cadillac,
And a set of 'Cycle' dishes
With his name embossed in black.

He even wore a set of hats
That a relative gave to me
And he looked like a Beagle-Businessman
As he modeled them handsomely!

There are so many memories
That I could here include
Of that chunky little canine
Who always searched for 'people food'.
But those which will always come to mind
As the years so swiftly fly
Are those that seemed so humorous
That I'd laugh until I'd cry:
The first was his search for rabbits
Which he never could quite snatch;
The second was the peanut butter
That in his mouth did 'catch'.

Oh, faithful friend, dear PANCHO,
I'll miss you through the years,
But your spirit will forever linger
Amidst the smiles and tears.

To take a quote from the Richie Ashburn journal: "OH, BROTHER!" How many people do you know whose family pets have uniforms of the local sports team? And tailor-made, no less!!

Another 'death' that occurred in my neighborhood in the early 1980's was that of some stately trees on the property of a neighbor. When the Borough employees drove up one morning and began to cut them down, I began to contemplate...

The Death of Shade and Foliage

I'd lived at Washington and Elm for nearly forty years
When I witnessed an activity that filled my eyes with tears.
I was seated in my kitchen when the incident began:
A borough truck drove up the street and from it stepped a man.
He was carrying a power saw and he climbed into a cage
That lifted him into the trees, as if walking on a stage.
And then he turned the power on and started cutting limbs
From the pair of greying giants (who now were whisp'ring hymns).
It didn't take him very long to end the giants' lives,
For the power that he wielded was much quicker than sharp knives.
Thus the limbs were quickly sliced apart and fell into the street
Where other men reduced them to sawdust piles so neat.

Those gentle leaf-filled giants had suffered much of late,
With ants that spread like cancer, as through the wood they ate,
And colonies of caterpillars eager to devour
The green and gorgeous foliage... a little more each hour.

The giants never groaned a lot as through the years they passed,
For in the shade beneath their limbs the ground was richly grassed.
And many were the memories stored deep within their roots-
Of heavy snows and neighbors' woes... and frigid canine snoots!

I know that I shall always see those gentle giants sway
In some bright tree-filled Paradise, where passing birds will say:
"How tall and strong and handsome are those sturdy leaf-filled trunks
That seem to wave a greeting... like two stately, pious monks."
But back at Washington and Elm an empty space now lies
Where once the beauty of those trees helped clean the hazy skies.
And though the space may disappear when new trees do appear,
The memory of those special friends will always be quite near.
For forty years of friendship can not soon be erased,
Since spirit stays long after the body's form is chased!

With this selection I bring to an end part three of my journey. I hope that I been able to provide you with some hints on how to 'preserve' those moments in time that have special meaning to you and those whom you love. Those diary entries, the fascinating photographs and the numerous newspaper clippings that we all collect during a lifetime of adventures can, indeed, become true treasures.

Mental images are also very important to our recollection of 'magical moments'. In the final part of my journey, I want to provide you with some of those images that combine elements of the future, the present and the past. As with any educator, the arrival of June signals a chance to 'escape', at least for a while, from the daily routine, and experience life from a different point of view. We all anticipate such moments, live them to the fullest and then look back on them with fond memories. The anxiety, the jubilation and the recollection processes associated with the experiences all work together to make the moments more enjoyable. Let's explore this great aspect of our lives, known as "R and R".

Part Four

**The Anticipation of,
the Participation in
and
the Contemplation of
Leisure Time Activities:**

<u>From Future to Present to Past</u>

Yes, indeed! Those anticipated days of "R and R" are close at hand. After ten months of ongoing activity, in the classroom, as adviser to extra-curricular groups and as volunteer in several community projects, I look forward to those few short weeks of Rest and Relaxation. Yet I find it somewhat difficult to put aside all of my work and experience 'true'...

Relaxation

How difficult it seems to be
To just relax (at least for me)
For, when I put my work aside,
My mind keeps trying to decide
If I should really cease my work-
Without becoming quite berserk-
By planning what I must soon do
As soon as relaxation's through!

It's obvious I can not rest
Because I want to do my best,
And relaxation can't occur
While mental cogs still want to stir.

So what is left for me to do?
I can't relax ; it makes me stew!
So I'll attempt to 'look' at ease.
Just don't make fun! And please don't tease!
For he who laughs at those like 'me'
Will NEVER rest... just wait and see!

The failure to 'unwind' has resulted in some interesting excursions into the realm of "mind games". One of the more fascinating of these "games" has been that of putting into verse various connotations of words in the English language. I am intrigued by the number of meanings often attached to a word, depending on the actual context in which it is used. I am able to gain a greater appreciation of the dilemma being faced by students who are attempting to learn to communicate in the English language as a result of my 'investigations'. Allow me to share one such dilemma with you.

I have chosen a word that I have used rather frequently in this collection of verse and have titled the selection ...

Time Rhymes

I have oft' TIMES thought a lot,
When having some TIME on my hands,
Of how TIME and TIME again I'd thought
Of TIME zones in different lands.
So it's now about TIME I set in print
What the TIME lag syndrome means,
For travelers must arrive on TIME...
Although lacking TIME machines.
If I don't get it right the first TIME
(And many TIMES I don't),
From TIME to TIME I'll rewrite it
Though a TIME clock punch I won't!

When a person asks: "What TIME is it?",
He or she must TIME it right.
For since TIME will wait for no man,
That TIME will vanish from sight.
And the only TIME we preserve it
Is when perfect TIMING shows-
Through TIME-lapse photos of it-
How the TIME zone passage slows.

Now since my TIME is precious,
And quite often I don't have TIME,
For the TIME being I'll just finish
This quite simple PASTIME rhyme...

What is my favorite PASTIME?
How do I spend my TIME?
If I had the TIME, I'd tell you,
But now's just not the TIME.
For now it's TIME for me to go
Just in the knick of TIME
To investigate the TIMELY facts:
Don't you think that it's about TIME ???

This TIME-killing poem was written on September 2, 1983, several days prior to the start of another school year. See what happens when an active educator has too much TIME on his hands??

But it would seem that I am getting ahead of myself. Let's return to June, that month in which I begin to contemplate my summer activities. Just before classes ended in 1991, I went out in my backyard one Saturday morning to feed some birds and found myself experiencing...

An Early Morning Takeoff

On the dew-covered lawn birds were waiting
As I slowly walked down the back steps.
Some were chirping "Good Morning",
While others a warning
Not to come up too close to the steps!

As the sky slowly brightened in sunlight,
From dark blue to a rose-colored hue,
I caught sight of a jet
Which the sunlight had met
To produce quite a picturesque view.
As the pilot banked left in his takeoff
To begin some routine, scheduled flight,
The plane shimmered in pink
Which, of course, made ME think
Of a lovely flamingo in flight.

As the jet disappeared in the distance,
After losing its colorful hue,
The birds on the ground
Now weren't making a sound...
Twas as if <u>they</u> the beauty could view.

When I later recalled that brief moment
Of uniqueness in sound and in light,
What at once came in view
Was that pink-colored hue
That had given me so much delight.

That unique 'sighting' of the jet taking off reminded me of an incredible August evening back in 1986 when a friend of mine and I decided to go to a PHILLIES game early in order to participate in one of the many giveaway promotions -- a giveaway that ended with...

A Fantasy Vacation

Twas the night of August 1st in 1986
When I drove to the VET and stood in line 'til 6
With 700 fans who had come to stand in line
In hopes of being lucky... for prizes there were nine!

The PHILLIES and a travel group had planned a night of fun,
With "Fantasy Vacations" for couples who had won:
A weekend spent in Boston, in Orlando or L.A.,
St. Louis, Kansas City or T A M P A...
And even in Seattle or Washington, D.C.
Or Phoenix, Arizona. Oh, what a fantasy!!!

I stood with travel bag in hand and number 505
Until, at 7:34, my spirit came alive:
They called the number 505 and then "ORLANDO" said...
And so I went to Florida before I went to bed.

What an unexpected surprise! While most of the fans who came to the giveaway brought enormous suitcases, I only had a small travel bag containing no clothing: only a toothbrush, an electric shaver and a camera. And while many of the winners did not leave Philadelphia until the next morning, the flight to Orlando was scheduled for an 8:15 pm takeoff. A limousine came onto the field, took me to the airport (after I found a place to park my car for the weekend) and took pictures of my friend and I as we ran through the airport in an effort to catch the flight. And you can probably imagine the reaction of my mother when I called her from the airport to tell her that I would see her in two days. I had to call her again from Orlando to explain all of the details.. because if I had tried to explain everything to her from the Philadelphia airport, we would have missed the flight. The PHILLIES gave us a copy of the videotape of our departure and, from time to time, I rerun it to relive that 'magical moment'.

Being a rather emotional individual, I tend to be somewhat more sensitive to activities occurring in nature than most. Especially during the summer months, I enjoy watching what goes on in the environment, whether at home or in some special vacation destination. There are times when ordinary happenings take on a special meaning for me and result in a poetic description of the 'event'.

One day, while sitting on a swing on my front porch, I became the observer of ...

A Day in the Life of a Spider

After building an intricate cobweb,
The spider then rested awhile...
'Til a fly became stuck in the webbing:
A sight which produced a curt smile.

She quickly preserved her new victim
In a casket of glis'ning white thread
And, after a peaceful 'siesta',
Entered into the casket and fed.
When her meal was at last fully eaten --
In two or three hours, or so --
She left once again by the webbing
To await sunset's last radiant glow.

As the stars began shining above her,
She returned... to start mending with care:
Spinning circles of thin silken webbing,
Suspended with great skill in mid air.

I observed all these actions with int'rest
And marvelled at what she had done.
For the patient and hard-working spider
Had a web which was magic'ly spun.
And I thought, as I watched her in silence:
What a perfect example is she
Of success in achieving objectives:
A fine model for both you and me!

As you can see from this description, success is not always easy to attain. It takes a lot of hard work, as well as patience. And, sometimes, success can be impeded because of a lack of understanding. You remember that earlier in our travels I mentioned the role of physical appearance and its role in our lives. This trait may also play an important role in nature. Take, for instance, the following situation that I observed in my backyard one summer morning. What I observed led me to think about the difficulties being faced by one tiger swallowtail butterfly in life, simply because it was...

A Butterfly with a Wrinkled Wing

My friends say that I'm handicapped because I'M not like they.
They flutter off when I come near, and with them I can't play.
But there is nothing wrong with me; there's just one minor thing:
I am a tiger swallowtail who has a wrinkled wing.

I fly as high and far as they, and pollinate as well...
But that one blemish on my wing does more than words can tell.
It labels me as something weird which doesn't fit the 'mold'...
And thus I'm forced to fly alone, through skies both warm and cold.

I know they'll never understand what damage they have done
By choosing not to fly with me... for they just think it's fun!
If only I could make them see that beauty is "wing deep",
While talent and ability are traits we ALL can reap!

But I'll not let them get me down and make me feel ashamed.
I'll simply work much harder to prove that I'm NOT maimed!
For I'm as good and strong as they, unique in just one thing:
I am that tiger swallowtail who has a wrinkled wing.

And you were thinking, perhaps, that discrimination was something that only applied to the human species? Guess again!

The inspiration for this poem came while I was watching several butterflies 'working' on a "butterfly bush" that is in my backyard. The swallowtail with the wrinkled wing was on one side of the bush, while six others were on the other side. As the 'unique one' moved around to the other side of the bush, all of the others flew away.

I consider this selection to be one of my best, for it seems to symbolize what often occurs in our daily lives. I have read it to several groups of poets at annual conventions, as well as to a group of EAST students at a special poetry reading session during an Arts Festival at the school. The feedback I have received from reading it has always been positive.

Because I tend to be sensitive to the role of nature in our lives, and because I get enjoyment from listening to the sounds of nature and viewing daily activities in it, I am constantly amazed by what appears to be a complete lack of interest on the part of many in these displays of Mother Nature. I believe that modern technology is partly responsible for this attitude. Take for example, the "walkman". The invention, and frequent use, of this piece of electronic 'wizardry' has caused me to consider the ongoing conflict between...

Mother Nature and the Walkman

A jogger went by me this morning
As I sat on my porch in a chair.
I was list'ning to sweet sounds of Nature,
But the jogger for them showed no care.
For he was wearing that confounded contraption
That technology made for us all:
That incredible 'toy' called the WALKMAN,
With cassette tapes and headset and all!

What a contrast this vision presented
As the Jogger moved on up the street...
Getting exercise outside with Nature,
Yet ignoring those sounds, soft and sweet,
Which, provided by dear Mother Nature,
Help us all to relax and unwind-
They were muffled by quaint little earphones,
Sending sounds of a much dif'rent kind.

The songs orchestrated by Nature
Are ignored by the Men of today
As they search for enjoyment and pleasure
In some new and mechanical way-
And 'relax' without list'ning to Nature
As they hustle to reach their next goal...
So, while striving to build up the body,
They've ignored leaving time for the soul!

How sad! Just as the slow-moving 'hands of TIME' have been replaced by the mechanical clicking of digital computation, the opportunities to 'stop and smell the flowers' have been lessened by the urgency of reaching some unknown destination 'on TIME'!

Even when we travel to distant places for relaxation, we can't survive without this mechanical "appendage" plugged into our ear 'sockets'. When I was in Maui in July of 1993, I was witness to several vacationers who were jogging along the beach BUT WITHOUT paying any attention to...

Nature's Song

Tennis players have arrived now at courtside
For an early morning match.
Several boats have set sail from the harbor
In search of some fish to catch.
Near the beach, where the palm trees are swaying,
Several joggers are running along,
While others are combing the beachfront
As WALKMEN serenade them in song.

But the song that I hear is quite different
From that of the WALKMAN's cassette:
It's a tune that's created by Nature
As her chorus our souls try to whet...
The breezes blow softly through palm fronds
To the beat of the incoming tide,
While the birds sing a cheerful good morning
As they, on the breezes, do glide.
The bees are 'a buzz' on the flowers
As they hum while caressing each bud,
And the frogs and the geckos sing praises
As the air, with their greetings, they flood.

I'm dismayed as I sit by the beachfront,
Watching those who ignore Nature's Song...
For they never place value on Nature
As on Life's Road they travel along.
And I fear that, as they grow older,
They'll regret what for years they ignored:
Taking time to enjoy Mother Nature-
They no time for such joy could afford!!

Join me now as I spend some time traveling to destinations near and far. As I mentioned earlier, I have been a 'Timeshare Traveler' since 1978 and have had many exhilarating experiences at resorts around the world. My favorite destinations have included New England, Southern California, Mexico (naturally, being a Spanish teacher) and Maui, Hawaii. But even close to home, one's senses can be aroused quite easily.

Many vacationers prefer to spend time at a lake or at the shore as a way to 'escape from daily routines'. There can be no doubt that there are many activities in which one can participate at such destinations: swimming, sunbathing, fishing, boating. Let's join in on the fun and excitement, beginning with a visit to...

The Lake

I went down to the lake late this morning
To observe one of Nature's great shows:
Schools of fish swimming by,
Flocks of birds on the fly,
Puffy clouds floating by, to and fro.

As I stood at the edge of the lakeshore,
Looking out on the picturesque scene,
Breezes whispered 'hello',
While the current below
Softly echoed their greeting serene.

And I watched as some boats left the lakeshore
Taking anglers out onto the lake...
While some children at play
Chased the birds in dismay.
What a marvelous film this would make!

So I sat on a bench near the lakeshore
To record what I'd seen on this day:
One of Nature's great sights,
Set aside for delights.
May it always remain just that way!

Let's now take a closer look at that pastime which provides relaxation AND exhilaration to so many of us: FISHING. Of course, we must remember that, while this is a sport for some, it represents much more than a recreational activity for many others: it is a way of life...

The Fishermen

The fishermen were standing on
The wooden Gulfport pier
With weighted nets
Not tossed in yet
To waters, oh, so clear.
For first, the fish are sighted
And observed while swimming by...
Then nets are tossed
With no time lost
To catch them from on high.
The nets descend to shallow depths
And close around the prey.
Then, hoisted high,
The mullets sigh
And struggle in dismay.

The fishermen stand once again
To peer into the sea...
Until they spy
More fish swim by-
And toss their nets with glee!

The joy of these old fishermen
Seems very rare these days...
To catch some fish
Fulfills their wish
For great success each day.

I wrote that poem in December, 1987 while on a winter vacation to Mississippi. Because I am NOT a lover of fishing, I was amazed at the enjoyment reflected in the eyes of the three fishermen who were standing on that wooden pier. I learned a lot about the sport in some brief conversations with them.

But did you know that all fishermen are NOT people??? Of course you did. However, just in case you may have forgotten, allow me to 'jog your memory' with this description of

The Pelican

Have you ever been sitting at the water's edge
As the sun slowly sets in the West,
Watching closely the moves of a pelican
That is soaring above some wave's crest?
Then you must be a friend of a fisherman
Who is constantly fishing the seas...
And who knows a great deal 'bout how well he can
Catch a meal with such style and such ease!

Oh, there's no greater show near the water's edge
Than the one oft' performed by the pelican,
As he proudly displays all his talents:
Swooping low, diving well, flying high again.
It's a scene from which novels are written,
Filled with love and desire and hope,
For the daily routine of the pelican
Shows us all how with Life we can cope.
There is patience and strength and agility
Seen in various moves that are made
By that awkward and clumsy big pelican:
He's ambitious, and never afraid!

When YOU next by the water's edge wander
In search of some sights rarely 'seen',
Take a moment to observe the proud pelican-
I'm quite certain you'll see what I mean!

As we all know, education is not limited only to the human race either. Examples of education occur in nature every day. I will give an example based on an experience I had in a visit to Atlantic City in July of 1990. If you have ever been on a boardwalk at a seaside resort, you have probably seen such an example of...

The Summer Lesson of Life

Dozens of seagulls
Diving toward the Boardwalk:
Feeding time has come.

Hundreds of tourists,
Walking along the Boardwalk,
Witness their approach.

Curious children,
Not knowing what is hap'ning,
Shout aloud with glee.

Some younger seagulls,
Frightened by the children's screams,
Scatter in dismay.

Others in the flock,
Anticipating handouts,
Land in search of food.

Local residents,
Aware of such mass landings,
Feed the hungry birds.

Timid young seagulls,
Observing what has happened,
Learn from their mistake.

Overstuffed seagulls,
Returning home with pleasure,
Talk of their success.

Children, now back home,
Discuss what they have witnessed:
A lesson in Life.

Once a teacher, always a teacher! It is fun, though, to see how learning can take place in various environments.

Another form of relaxation that involves visits to "shorelines" is the game of golf. Did I say RELAXATION?? How can a golfer relax?.... especially when faced with the constant threat of loss of property? How many golf balls have YOU seen submerge beneath the surface of some nearby water hazard? ...That many?? WOW!! Have you ever stopped for a moment to view the game of golf from its point of view?? You haven't? Please allow me to introduce you to my good friend...

The Water Hazard

As the sun comes up each morning
And penetrates the haze,
It reflects upon my surface-
And the golfers does amaze.
But soon that reflection's shattered
As the golf balls head my way
And cause gigantic ripples,
As well as great dismay.

Some insects come and drink from me
As the hours roll on by:
Some are caught by fish below;
Some caught by birds on high.
By sunset I have swallowed up
A hundred balls or more...
And golfers, with their magic wands,
My waters do explore
In efforts to retrieve a few
For use in future rounds-
While I endure those futile prods
And muffled human sounds.

When all the golfers fin'ly leave,
Some ducks come for a swim...
And snack on surface tidbits
(Which, at times, are rather slim.)

When night arrives, the Moon appears
And shines upon my face,
While stars reflect their wondrous forms
From far in outer space.

A water hazard's life is tough,
But I shall ne'er complain,
For ev'ry day brings some surprise...
In sunshine or in rain:
Some smiling face looks down on me
And grins from ear to ear,
While birds and fish and insects
Gather 'round from far and near.
It makes existence bearable
As days turn Into years...
Especially when I'm looked upon
With anguish and with sneers!

So next time you approach my edge
And stare into my depths,
Remember that I'm looking back,
Reflecting all your steps.
Please try to wave or even smile,
In spite of what you've lost!
For smiles bring joy and happiness,
Regardless of the cost!!

What a friend! And talk about success!! A water hazard may collect a fortune in colorful round 'trinkets' on a busy weekend!

Speaking of the 'cost' of happiness conjures up images of bills piling up following an extended vacation at a destination far from home. Those of you who have taken a long vacation know what I mean, right? You are also VERY familiar with the adventures associated with being...

Vacation Bound

Vacation time is here at last,
A time for R and R.
But getting to the chosen spot...
By plane, and then by car...
Will take up almost one full day--
With precious hours spent
Just waiting for the airport van,
And wond'ring where it went!...
Then going through the hassle
In the airport check-in line:
With baggage tags and boarding pass
And seats oft' reassigned!

What follows is the lengthy walk
To find departure gates,
Complete with more inspections
And, then, extended waits
For some set flight departure
Which oft' becomes delayed...
Resulting in a state of mind
Produced by nerves quite 'frayed'.

But arrival time does fin'ly come:
It's time to claim the bags
And prove those bags are really yours,
By handing in the tags...
Which now are prob'ly put away
With other ref'rences,
In jacket pocket envelopes:
The traveler's nemesis!

At last you're free to stand in line
To get a rental car--
Provided you have brought along
Some proof of who you are!
You need to have a credit card
To pay for what you choose,
And validated license...
Which the agent will peruse
Before assigning you a car
And giving you advice
On how to find your way around.
Now THAT is really nice!

A tourist van now takes you to
The car YOU chose to drive.
And what a shock awaits you-
For goodness sake's alive!
The agent didn't give advice
On how to DRIVE the car,
And you can't seem to figure out
Where certain features are...
Like how to turn the headlights on,
Or readjust the seat,
Or locate where the button is
That regulates the heat!

Ah! Fin'ly you have reached the spot
You chose for 'R and R'.
The time has come to have some fun...
But did you lock the car??
Have fun, vacation-seeker,
But keep in mind ... beware....
For half the fun of 'R and R'
IS IN THE GETTING THERE

I could feel some of you 'trembling' as you relived these "magic moments". But flying to a vacation destination can be exciting AND breathtaking, especially if you take time to look out the window from 30,000 feet and look down upon those charming...

Model Towns

We had just leveled off, six miles above ground,
On a breathtaking flight to O'Hare
In the Midwestern city, Chicago:
In a short time we'd be landing there.
As I looked out the window at the clouds passing by
I could see quite a lot down below:
There were houses and highways and numerous farms...
And thousands of lawns yet to mow.

The view from the window made me feel like a child
Whose parents had given much joy
With a marvelous present-a miniature town-
What a wondrous and magical toy!
I could see the toy autos on the miniature roads
As they scurried along, just like ants...
And the little toy vessels in those rivers so small
As like corks on the ocean they'd dance.
There were miniature golf courses scattered about,
And those miniature buildings and pools.
I remembered how I used to organize towns
On the carpet, without any tools.

It's amazing the images that pass through one's mind
When one looks at a town from above,
But what brings one joy as he relives such scenes
Is that mem'ries are triggered by Love!

And as the towns continue passing by below, hidden at times by some clouds, the traveler may be fortunate enough to catch sight of a...

Sunset from Above the Clouds

The clouds below the streaking jet
Looked just like desert sand,
With some dark columns rising up
Like pillars from the land.
And, as the sun began to set
Behind some distant clouds,
Those columns took on strange new shapes,
From walls to rocks to shrouds.
They caused the light to be dispersed
In strange and eerie ways...
From velvet hues of crimson red
To somber, ghostly greys.

From just inside the streaking jet
I looked upon the scene-
As a patron at the theatre looks
With eyesight, oh so keen-
And saw the sun begin to hide,
Descending through the clouds,
Then disappear behind the wing,
Escaping from the crowds.

And high above the streaking jet
The evening star appeared,
Protruding like a 'Guiding Light'...
The sun had disappeared.
Yet, far off in the western sky,
The sun's last light still shone,
Reflecting off the billowed clouds
Like arrows weakly thrown.
The brilliant shades of crimson red
Had dulled as darkness fell...
Converted into ghostly shades
Which silent death foretell.

The clouds below the streaking jet
No longer could be seen
As darkness fell across the sky,
That now looked so serene.
The three-act play was now complete
And stars had filled the sky...
Like lights within the theatre
As the patrons say good-by.
The sun provided quite a show
While setting in the West,
And those of us who watched it
Felt we'd seen its very best!

What a breathtaking way to begin a vacation! And when a person is traveling, it is often amazing to discover how friendly and how helpful complete strangers can be. They answer questions, provide advice on places to dine, recommend special places to visit, etc. Following a nice conversation with a couple in Cape Cod, Massachusetts in early 1993, I was reminded of those interesting situations involving...

Strangers and Friends

It's so often we speak with a stranger,
And so seldom we speak with a friend,
As we travel around
Towards sites never found
Caught between the beginning and end
Of a journey that's filled with excitement
And adventures we ne'er can foresee.
Our success will depend,
Not on some longtime friend
But some stranger who responds to our plea...
For assistance in finding a highway
Or advice on the best place to eat...
As we search far and near,
Week by week, year by year,
For that road to some longed-for retreat.
It's so odd how our friends seem like strangers
While those strangers, like some long-lost friends
As the days turn to years
And our smiles turn to tears
As our journey follows roads with no ends.
When we finally reach the last highway,
And our lifetime of searching is through,
We look back with regret,
For we've come to forget
All those strangers who were friends, tried and true.

And speaking of strangers and strange situations reminds me of an experience I had while driving through Massachusetts on my way back to New Jersey. I became lost and, in an effort to relocate the right highway, found myself being helped by...

The Road With No Name

There's a short stretch of highway
In a large New England state
That connects two major roadways:
And it really is 'first rate'!

Its surface makes the trip a joy
And the scenic views are great!
There are frequent signs to guide you
And you never have to wait...
For traffic lights to change to green
Or Rotary tie-ups to end!

I enjoyed my travels on it.
It could be called a friend.
But there is one thing missing
That my conscience does offend:
This highway doesn't have a NAME!!
Could this be some new trend??
The road signs tell you what's ahead
And clearly show the way,
But nothing tells you 'who' it is,
So what will people say
When pointing out this stretch of road
They travel on each day? ......
"IT carries you from here to there
With never a delay!"

I'd like to write a brief complaint
To those who built this road.
I feel so sad that I could cry,
Or with angry words explode!...
For they have been quite careless
And have failed in what is owed:
A NAME for that great surface
That carries well each load!!

How sad that such an important stretch of highway has no proper identification. But there are other examples of sites that no longer have importance to the lives of those who live near them. Several years ago, while traveling Northeast on Route 33 on the way to the Poconos, I caught sight of...

The Silent Silo

As I drove to the Pocono Mountains,
Going northeast on Route 33,
Just by chance I caught sight of a silo
That is now just a sad memory
Of a time when it served a proud farmer
By preserving those tons of fine grain,
Long produced on the fields of the farmland
As a source of some financial gain,
Or for use by the farmer as fodder
For the livestock that grazed on the farm.
What a glorious view of a lifestyle
That conveyed both hard work and quaint charm!

But that silo's now covered in ivy
That has crept up its stately tall frame
After years of neglect by NEW owners
Who are constantly placing the blame
For the present poor state of the silo
On some strange economic decline...
Which will soon put an end to a symbol
Of an era which once was so fine.

Let's travel West now and take a look at some sites in Southern California. I travel to this part of the country twice a year because I have several Timeshares at the Lawrence Welk Villas in Escondido, some 35 miles north of San Diego on Route 15. There are always many things to do at this resort, but the vacationer can also spend his or her time lounging at poolside or watching the golfers on one of the resort's two courses. Allow me to describe...

A Day at Lawrence Welk Villas

The sun comes up and calls to me
In my Escondido suite:
"Don't lie in bed all day, my friend!
Get up and move those feet!"

At Lawrence Welk's renowned resort
There's much that you can do:
There's tennis, golf and games galore,
Plus a 'Music Theatre', too.
And so I rise and start my day
By swimming in the pool,
Or just relaxing in my suite
In the shade where it is cool-
On my patio in 316
I have a wondrous view
Of a golf course fairway and its green,
And a water hazard, too!

Of course, I could participate
In exercise routines,
Held daily for an hour
For adults, as well as teens.
And then, there's TIJUANA
On a day trip filled with fun!
It's a trip across the border
And a treat for everyone!

I could, of course, walk to DEER PARK,
With its classic car museum,
And stroll through scenic vineyards:
You really oughta see 'um!!!

Each night there's something special
For the guests to come and see:
There's BINGO, or a concert,
Or a "Murder Mystery".
One night there is a Bar-B-Q
With lots and lots of food,
And YES, an evening social
With a real romantic mood.

And so each night I thank the sun
For calling me each day:
This Escondido Paradise
Is tops in ev'ry way!!

Have you played any BINGO lately?? You haven't??? You don't know what you're missing!! Everyone needs to experience the excitement of...

Bingo

B is for the board on which we play it,
I for ingenuity of play,
N for one less number to encounter,
G for grins of joy that some display,
O is for the order of the contests

Designed to keep the competition keen
Until, at last, there comes the cry of "BINGO",
That sound that signals victory serene.

And who, you ask, will play this little board game
In hopes of shouting out the winning sound?
It's EVERYONE, because no skill is needed:
It's a game in which real pleasure can be found!

Wow! Let's play a game of 'blackout'!

Of course, whenever anyone mentions Lawrence Welk, the first thing that comes to mind is that famous expression made popular by this musician and band leader...

"Ah One and Ah Two and Ah..."

The title of this poem
Brings some vivid thoughts to mind
Of entertaining music
Of a very special kind!
It helps recall the mem'ries
Of that "Champagne Music Man"
Who gave so much enjoyment
To each and every fan.
His name of course is Lawrence,
He's the leader of the band
That captured many hearts and souls
Across our scenic land.
The rhythm of the "Champagne-style"
Will live forever more,
So many thanks, dear Lawrence Welk
For those mem'ries by the score!!

As I mentioned in the first poem about the Lawrence Welk Villas, one of the weekly activities is a day trip to TIJUANA, MEXICO. My participation in one of these trips gave me the opportunity to practice my Spanish and also to observe...

A Different Way of Life

I walked the Tijuana streets
And browsed in many shops
In search of tiny souvenirs...
From books to children's tops.
But what, for ME, stands out the most
Of all I saw that day
Was watching sev'ral youngsters work,
Instead of merely play.
One boy was playing his guitar
And singing Spanish songs.
His friend played an accordion
While singing right along.
Both boys were only eight or nine
And could not play too well,
But playing was the only 'gift'
That they could hope to sell.
The way in which those two boys played
And sang, to earn some cash,
Reminded me how poor they were
AND how two cultures clash!
For San Diego County lies Just North of Tijuana,
But Life "South of the Border style"
Indeed IS Mexicana.

I enjoyed that day in Tijuana, for it allowed me to view firsthand the daily life of the residents in that border town. I have visited several other destinations in Mexico since 1980. Early in 1992, I spent some time vacationing in the city of MAZATLAN, on the West coast of the country. While there, I was able to view some...

Joys of Early Morning

I watch as the sun ushers in a new day,
Then follow the butterflies in brilliant display,
Overhear conversations of birds in the palms,
Sense the joy of all Nature as it soothes and it calms,
Feel the touch of the breeze as it softly wafts by,
Smell the fragrance of flowers which the breeze lifts on high,
Touch the droplets of dew on the glistening grass,
Spot some playful crustaceans on the beach as I pass,
See the algae afloat on the incoming tide,
Speak to seagulls and pelicans as on updrafts they glide,
Reach up to the Heavens and silently pray,
Then rejoice as a witness to Nature's display...
For I'm blessed with the senses through which I explore
All of Nature's great beauty-and expressions galore-
As I walk and observe, to my mind's great delight,
What most take for granted in the dawn's early light.

Have you ever awakened before dawn and taken a stroll along the beach? If so, I'm certain that you are familiar with those 'joys of early morning'. If not, I would encourage you to try it some time (without the walkman, of course). The experience will provide you with relaxation beyond your wildest expectations.

Let's now travel to my favorite destination: MAUI, Hawaii. I recently purchased a Timeshare on the Kihei coast of Maui, located only two blocks from the MAUI SUNSET, the resort that I visited back in 1980. The property is the MAUI SCHOONER and is owned in part by the Welk organization. What a Paradise!! And there are so many new and exciting things to see on this island. One of these is a truly unique phenomenon that results from the burning of sections of the fields of sugarcane. For me, a genuine 'joy of early morning' occurred when I stepped out on my lanai and discovered some physical evidence of...

Sugarcane Rain

I awakened quite early one morning,
And was startled by what I did see:
Black cinders had covered the lanai!
Now, what in the world could it be?

When I opened the door to the lanai,
I could smell something strange in the air...
And, since I don't live in Hawaii,
I could with it not one thing compare.
As the breeze began blowing more strongly,
A strange cloud slowly passed overhead:
It was dense and like caramel in color,
Yet its "moisture" was blacker than lead!
When I tried to examine the cinders,
They disintegrated right in my hand...
Yet the grass and the lanai were covered
With a coating of this dusty black "sand"!

It was then that I finally realized
What was hap'ning around me that morn:
They were burning a section of cane field...
That's where those black cinders were born!
For the sugarcane harvest in Maui
Begins with the fields set ablaze,
But for tourists who don't know what's hap'ning,
The resulting 'black rain' will amaze...
For they've all heard of showers on Maui,
But they are known as sweet "pineapple rain".
How amazing to see those black showers
Which I now know is burnt sugarcane.

The scenic beauty of Maui. This panorama greets the visitor as he or she travels from the airport to Kihei.

The hula is a dance that embraces the Aloha spirit. The movements of the hands tell stories of the history of the Hawaiian people. These young Hawaiians are helping to preserve that history in song and dance.

The flower lei is one of Hawaii's most beautiful traditions. Whether given or worn, it embodies the meaning of "Aloha" and specializes an occasion. It says "welcome" (as when presented to vacationers upon arrival to the islands), "I love you", "Congratulations", or is a form of dressing up.

One of Mother Nature's finest displays of color and beauty occurs each evening at sunset. As the sun sets into the sea off the Kihei coast of Maui, there is a special feeling of 'Aloha' experienced by all observers. The view is breathtaking and what makes it so very special is that no two are ever alike.

Marvelous experiences in another cultural setting! And the citizens of the islands continue to keep tradition alive in a variety of ways. One of the most beautiful of these traditions is the hula, a dance performed daily for visitors. It is not only fascinating to watch, but also very meaningful, especially to those who well understand the significance of each of those...

Maui Movements

Native performers,
Proud of their rich heritage,
Help traditions live.

Young hula dancers,
Dressed in colorful attire,
Dance with hips and hands.

Gently swaying hips,
Combined with silent language
Of the dancer's hands,
Beckon us to watch
As history comes alive
In Maui movements.

Older performers
Translate every movement-
Help us understand.

Let's understand them
And LEARN, from Maui movements,
How history lives!

There I go, sounding like a teacher again. Can't I just learn to relax, without seeing some 'hidden meaning' in everything? I don't know if I can or not. I think I must be a romantic, for I am always searching for beauty and meaning as I sit and observe what is taking place around me. Even a beautiful Maui sunset makes me think about an orchestra that is playing some prelude in an opera house, prior to the appearance of the performers (the stars). There's anticipation followed by incredible exhilaration as one observes Mother Nature as she performs for her audience on an...

Evening in Paradise

As the sun slowly sets behind the West Maui Mountains
And another day in Paradise ends,
Palm trees sway in the breeze
While the visitor sees
What a message Mother Nature now sends!
First the sky changes color, from a brilliant light blue
To a mixture of yellow and red;
Then the yellow succumbs
to what quickly becomes
A magnificent display, softly spread,
Of a deep reddish-orange, with a yellowish hue,
Which immediately changes once more
To a deep reddish glow,
From above and below...
Just the prelude to what lies in store.

The first brilliant light to appear in the sky
Is that heavenly body of love.
And, as Venus shines bright,
There soon follows more light
From the thousands of stars up above!

As I sit on a lanai on a Kihei resort,
Watching all of these changes unfold,
I'm so glad I can say
At the end of each day:
"What a wondrous sight to behold!"

What a wondrous sight indeed! And speaking of wondrous sights, have YOU ever been fortunate enough to be an eyewitness to a total solar eclipse?? You haven't?? Well, I <u>almost</u> was... on the island of MAUI on Thursday morning, July 11, 1991. Observers from all over the world came to the island that week to witness...

The Solar Eclipse of 1991

On the island of MAUI
On the eleventh of July
An event long predicted
Took place in the sky...
As the Moon showed its power
By eclipsing the Sun,
Turning daylight to twilight
Before it was done!
But for those who had waited
To view the great sight,
Many dreams turned to nightmares
During "dawn's early light"...
For the two-hour program,
Pre-arranged for us all,
Was kept hidden by Nature,
Who arranged for a squall!!

There were clouds and thick fog
Over all of the isle,
So that no one could see IT
For even a while.
The eclipse was detected
By a darkening sky,
But the Moon's great performance
Wasn't seen by the eye!

I was there when it happened,
I was out on a boat...
Getting drenched by the downpour,
Trying hard not to gloat.
For I'd sensed what was hap'ning
As the temperature dropped...
And an eerie grey color
Proved that sunlight had stopped!

I was thrilled by the moment,
I and 23 more,
Who, with Bruce, Buck and Kelly
Tried the gods to implore
To provide us a "window"
Through which we might see
The Sun's bright corona
From our seats on the sea!
We prepared our SUNPEEPERS
And drank some champagne,
While enjoying our 'fieldtrip'
In the wind and the rain.

I SHALL NEVER FORGET IT!!
What more can I say?
For, though I saw nothing,
I enjoyed the whole day!!!

I videotaped this incredible adventure on the rough seas off the Kihei coast in Maui. The captain of the boat on which we spent more than eight hours (we departed from the harbor at 5:15 am) said that he had never experienced weather conditions like those of July 11, 1991 in more than 25 years of sailing around the island. Obviously, Mother Nature was 'queen' that day.

Dining can be another fascinating experience on Maui. One location that is 'truly Hawaiian' is Mama's Fish House, located in Paia on the road that leads to Hana (where Lindbergh's grave is located). Mama's offers the diner an opportunity to experience...

Beachfront Dining

What a setting for a great seafood dinner,
Near PAIA on Route 36,
Nestled snugly in tropical beauty:
One of MAUI's top restaurant picks.
The name of the spot: MAMA'S FISH HOUSE
And, inside, the motif is unique.
The decor is completely Hawaiian,
With some idols of jade and of teak.
On the walls are artistic reminders
Of the culture to which you're exposed...
From the beauty of picturesque artwork
To shell necklaces on beams stately posed.
During dinner you're treated to music
That is strictly Hawaiian in style,
And the cuisine is quite varied and "ono"...
Making choices may take you a while.
There are ten ways to order an entree,
Maybe grilled, perhaps baked or sauteed,
And the freshness of all of the seafood
Makes the meal worth the price that is paid.
From the wine list and choice of great cocktails
To the loaf of just-baked, homemade bread,

From delicious fish chowder or salad
To some cake (or some ice cream instead),
Every course is prepared to perfection
And the service is "A NUMBER 1"...
With a staff that knows just what is needed
From the moment it greets everyone.

There's much more I could say about MAMA'S,
It is truly a dining delight.
But you'll never find out 'til you've been there...
Now 'bout going for dinner tonight!!

    MAMA'S is just one of many oceanfront restaurants located on the island and quite a few offer Hawaiian music as a background for dining. Several places combine a buffet meal with a special live program of Hawaiian and Polynesian entertainment. One of the most outstanding of these is the MAUI LU Resort in Kihei, where a fabulous show is presented by Mr. Maui...

Jesse Nakooka

I was talking with Jesse Nakooka
In the MAUI LU Longhouse Cafe
And was asking him about all the music
That he sang and on piano did play.
In Hawaii he is called Mr. MAUI,
And it's easy to understand why:
For his voice is as soft as the tradewinds,
Yet as strong as a kite flying high,
Reaching up for the clouds, swiftly passing,
In the vibrant and blue Kihei sky
As it touches the soul and the heartstrings
Of those lucky to be passing by.
For the people who listen to Jesse
Are indeed like those clouds up above
Who are touched by his magical singing
That is filled with emotion and love.
And, as they return to their homelands,
They carry a feeling unique
That echoes the heartbeat of Maui:
Jesse gave them what they'd come to seek!

What impressed me the most about Jesse
Was his love for the work that he does
As he talks about why he's performing
AND the joy in presenting what was...
In an effort to continue tradition
And present that of which he is proud
In a way that invites us to join him
By singing his message aloud.
There's the beautiful song about weddings
And the tunes telling us where he's at,
And the tender reminders of childhood...
And of weaving a coconut hat.

Here's to JESSE, indeed, MR. MAUI,
May he long bring us moments of joy
As he serenades list'ners with feeling
And reveals what he'd learned as a boy
Growing up on the island of Maui
In a quaint, picturesque whaling town,
Then presenting his shows down in Kihei,
Where he reigns as performer renowned.

At the end of each day, I return to my lanai and look up into the star-filled skies. Having lived my entire life just outside of Philadelphia, where the city lights make it impossible to experience the beauty of a sky containing millions and millions of lights twinkling down from above, I find myself enthralled by the nightly....

Hawaiian Sky Drama

As I stood out on the lanai
Of a Maui island suite
Watching moonset over Kihei-
The day's last brilliant feat-
I stared into the heavens
Where the twinkling stars abound,
And thought I heard them speaking...
Though I couldn't hear a sound!
For the sky was like a backdrop
Used as setting for a play,
And the stars the budding actors
Putting on their proud display...
Of outfits gleaming in the lights,
Of voices taut with fear
In great anticipation
Of the audience's cheer.

But were those stars just bits of light
A twinkling in the skies?
Or were they spirits so sublime
Which, with winking of their eyes,
Encourage me to wonder
And to dream away my cares?
And even offer challenges,
Or perhaps just answer prayers?

The moonset now completed,
I returned to solid ground
And marveled at the feelings
Which in their play I'd found.
And, as I left the lanai
I glanced once more above
To watch those actors winking
From their wondrous stage of Love.

Is it any wonder that I consider MAUI my favorite destination... in spite of the twelve to fourteen hours of travel required to get there from New Jersey? But... what ELSE can be found on MAUI (other than hula dancers, beautiful sunsets and the remnants of burnt sugarcane)? Allow me to summarize in a 'poem' for which I received Honorable Mention in the Summer 1992 Awards Program from Iliad Press. Not surprisingly, the title of the selection is...

Maui

Clear
Blue skies
Swaying palms
Cooling tradewinds
Agile windsurfers
Frisbee tossers
Kite flyers
Lanais
Peace

Bright
Sunshine
Moonlit nights
Fragrant flowers
Flowing waterfalls
Cooling Mai-Tais
Paradise
MAUI
Isle

I am sure that you can understand my love for this island paradise. When I first visited Maui, I wrote my thoughts in the form of a wish. The poem won fifth place in the 1985 National Amateur Poet Search, sponsored by the Johnson Publishing Company. I longed to be a cirrus cloud in order to enjoy...

A Fleeting Glimpse of Paradise

Oh, to be a cirrus cloud,
Above the Maui cane,
Floating, oh so softly,
So near the Kihei plain
Amidst the gently-blowing palms
Which grow and sway with ease...
In air that's swept by tradewinds
Which all their fronds do tease.

My life would be so carefree
As I floated to and fro,
Just puffing up from time to time
As near the hills I'd go.
And though my life would be quite brief
In the sunlit Maui skies,
I'd vanish quite contentedly,
No sadness in my eyes,
And fall upon the Kihei coast
As sweet pineapple rain...
For I'd have been a cirrus cloud
Above the Maui cane!

And so ends a journey along the road of life with a romantic educator. I hope that my adventures have provided you, the reader, with some enjoyment... as well as with some 'food for thought'. Life does offer each of us many opportunities to observe and to explore. We must, of course, prepare well for our investigations and be aware that, from time to time, we will be faced with situations that were not anticipated. If we show determination and maintain our focus on set goals, we will all be able to share in the exhilaration that comes from the fulfillment of our dreams.

Did you know that I have been observing you as you have read this collection of poems? You didn't?? Then you had better continue reading and see what I have to say in my...

Afterword

So YOU are that reader of poems
Who was searching around for some clues!
Well, did I succeed
In meeting your need
For direction-with 'signs' you could use?

For you see, I'm that writer of poems
Who enjoys writing verses in rhyme
Which, when placed in print,
Give others a hint
As to what can be done with their time!

And THIS was that small book of poems
That awaited the chance to be read...
In the hope that the lines
Would provide some sure signs
Of adventures still lying ahead.

I sure hope it's a happy reunion
That resulted from reading this text.
May all that you do
Make YOUR dreams come true...
As each success leads to the next!

For then I'd be that writer of poems
Who'd made readers so much more content...
Though he never knew
That some dreams had come true
Thanks to thoughts which in poems he'd sent.

Best wishes for success and happiness always!